Sorry, We're Close

J. Tarin Towers

Manic D Press
San Francisco

Thanks to the following publications, where some of these poems appear in slightly different forms: 9x9 Industries Broadsides series (1998 and 1997); *The Pushcart Prize Anthology XXIII*; *The Rag*; *Denatured Birds & Reincarnation Names: The 1997 San Francisco Slam Team Anthology*; *The Fray*; *Mouth: The Best of the San Francisco Word Scene*; *Pocket Anthology: The 1998 Albuquerque Poetry Festival*; *Beaten to the Bone*; *New Mission News*; *The New Bull Horn*; *San Francisco Bay Guardian*; *6,500*; and the chapbook, *No Shame*.

Cover illustration: Mary Fleener
Cover design: Scott Idleman/BLINK

Library of Congress Cataloging-in-Publication Data

Towers, J. Tarin.
    Sorry we're close / J. Tarin Towers.
    p. cm.

ISBN 0-916397-58-0 (alk. paper)
I. Title.
PS3570.O878 S67 1999
811'.54--dc21
                          99-6285
                          CIP

Contents

10   Apocalypso #1

11   Apocalypso #1, Part 2

Guns 'N' Things

15   The Hitchers, #3

16   Ace Hardware

20   How To Get A Good Night's Sleep

22   Making Mistakes

25   Mission Poem

26   I'm Not Easy

28   Pepper Spray

31   The Thinking Problem

34   Good Listener

36   Legend in My Own Mind

39   Smack (1998 Nostalgia Remix)

Love Has Always Been My Game

43   What I Did Today

44   Collecting Box Tops

46   What They Leave

47   To Forget

49   Psych Study

52   Phantom Limb

55   Discount Pulse Rate

58   Letter

59   "I Love You" Poem

61   Thorn

63   Analogy

66   April 1995, or What I Thought About

68   2-point Conversation

70   Afterwards

Shallow Water No Diving

75   Sonnet

76   Epitaph

77   One Night Standoff

79   Abecedarian: Ask Bobby

80   Oral Fixation

82   Picky

84   Walter

85   How To Break Up With Your Boyfriend

87   Punk Rock Boy

88   Judas Was a Girl

89   Abridged Virgin

93   February 3, 1995

94   Three Observations on Belief

95   Dumps

98   Bus Transfer Poem #3

We Apologize for Any Convenience

101   Samantha

102   Junk Drawer

104   For the Birds

106   Book

109   Don't I Know You

111   In-Just Spring

113   Behind the Bar

116   Dear Jay

There are plenty of reasons not to throw yourself off a bridge.
Some of those reasons are my friends, and this is for them.
(Another reason is that you probably won't
spontaneously combust underwater, but that's covered elsewhere.)

"Some things can't be ravished. You can't ravish a can of sardines."
—D.H. Lawrence, *Lady Chatterley's Lover*

"The universe is expanding, but we aren't getting any farther apart."
—David Fox, *Thanks for the Heads Up*

Apocalypso #1

He kissed me
Right on the apocalypse,

and said, "Never, ever
forget me."

"I won't," I said.
"I can't," I said.

The world is ending,
and I will never forget anything

again.

Apocalypso #1, Part 2

He thought I was hell
on wheels but really
I was purgatory
riding around in a shopping cart
with one bum wheel.

A well-oiled machine shop.
Butter wouldn't melt.
The saints went marching out.
It was a spade,
so we called it a cab.

Guns 'N' Things

The Hitchers, #3

Yesterday we left to look
for a garage to hold
our bodies and bags
of belongings — two books, etc.

Just stick out your thumb and say aah.
Just stick out your neck.
When the mail train comes,
the hook will get it.
The hook always gets it.

When we got here we stopped
watching for cars.
Which is how you died.
Not watching.
The cars did the rest.
I almost walked home.
They would have taken me back.
But 500 miles will never be enough.

Ace Hardware

Ace is the place with the helpful hardware man. —Ace Hardware Jingle

I just spent $277 and 78¢ at Ace Hardware
because I had a fight with my boyfriend this morning.
Tearful and fretful, I went from my apartment
to the coffee shop, read science fiction
vindictively for three hours, dropped off
some terribly urgent Priority Mail at the Post Office,
and headed to the ALA Convention.

I am not a librarian, although I have spent
my share of hours saying "shhh" to cranky children.
I am here as a writer, performing the utmost
in white collar crimes: impersonating a librarian.
I'm wondering if Alice, whose badge I'm pinned to,
could get disbarred, or dis-barcoded, for this.

I skink around the booths at Moscone Center—
the multimedia displays, I should say.
There is more silicon in this room
than at a Playboy Bunny alumni reunion.
Weighted down with catalogs and bookmarks,

I disembark and skirt Yerba Buena Gardens,
home to artsy acid droppers and well-dressed
homeless veterans, headed for hardware.
All I want are a few hooks and nails.

Until I see the Mikita aisle. The Mikita
is not a twittering poisonous insect,
but the very best name in cordless
power drills and power screwdrivers.
I have some things to hang.

I go up and down the aisles of Ace
more skillfully than Safeway's.
I buy gadgets and blades,
brushes and hammers, paint,
paint thinner, nails, hooks,
and a few more hooks.

Hooks are all-purpose. I have
some things to hang. I charge
tools like a lottery winner,
trying to forget I did this
just last week, in the not-dissimilar
islands of Victoria's Secret.
They were having a sale.

Waiting for BART, I witness
BART's own IQ test in action.
The announcer declares that two trains
are bound for Daly City. One will reach
Embarcadero in four minutes. Another,
two cars shorter, is close behind,

expected here at Powell in five.
When four minutes pass, a covey
of watches beep, and two dozen
Asian men look expectantly,
smugly, at their wrists.

The promised train for Daly City
arrives in four point four minutes,
filled to the armpits with yuppies
wrapping up the daily grind.

Maybe you're smart enough
to program that watch, I think,
but we'll see who has a better train
ride home. I lean on the wall,
watching the suits sardine themselves

into the Tin Can Express, holding
poles like bottles of Evian.
One minute later, a sparsely
populated Daly City train pulls in,
and I sit in a comfy seat, joining
the smartest BART passengers alive.

On the way home, I use Shit Alley
to avoid the sidewalk sales. Two

Mexican men, eyeing my drill,
ask me if I can change their battery.
"I left my allen wrench at home,"
I smile, leaving them baffled.
It's just as well. That would give

Mr. Harrington, the Irish antiques
magnate, who speaks in tongues
Sunday mornings on Mission Street,
a chance to pirate my new Mikita.
He'd spray on some bottled patina
and axle grease, and sell it promptly

as a vintage drill. I am proud of my
purchases, as proud as I was after
my first trip to Good Vibrations.
I think of the guy who helped me
pick out my drill—cute, really—

congratulating me on my buy.
"You may want to take those
labels off," he said, "so no one
knows what's in that box."

"Well," I grinned, "everyone's
afraid of a girl with a power
drill," and he dematerialized.
I never saw him again.
So as I hit the corner of 17th,

I compose a poem in my head:
"Nothing sets a man's heart shaking
like a girl with a drill who pumps iron."
Just then, a woman—looks like a
legitimate ALA escapee—says,
"Excuse me, but I couldn't help

remarking on the slogan on your
t-shirt, especially in light of your
bags." I dimly realize what my

ad for the day is, a relic of an
Ani DiFranco concert:
"Every tool is a weapon,
if you hold it right." I blush.

"New weapons," she chuckles.
"I'll use them wisely," I tell her.
I retreat into my building,
passing the nicklers, dimers,
quarterers, and dollarers,
and check my mail.

The new Victoria's Secret catalog
is here already. And me without
a spoon. I start drilling immediately,
wondering if these batteries
are rechargeable. I screw the wall

open and shut like a mouth,
giving new homes to mirrors,
shelves, pictures of home.
I have some things to hang.

How To Get A Good Night's Sleep

Light goes so fast it doesn't even
notice; so do we. Can't sleep? Wake
up then. It's always in the last place
you look, and what are you searching
for? Money? More time? Less work
or more work or better? Leave these
thoughts behind the garage they came
out of; you can't drive somewhere
safe if it's the end of the world
you're afraid of. Do what I do.

Don't sell your car, take it apart
with a jigsaw. Every place is the same
"there" when you think you're
nowhere. Plant the pieces like pot
seeds in public gardens and city
parks. Steal some roach traps, drive
those instead. What goes in never comes
back out, and that's what you wanted,
a sense of closure. Am I right?

Break your watch. Undo the clasp,
place it on concrete and stomp
stomp stomp till it couldn't think
of ticking. Forget licking, take
hammer if need-be to its glossy
crystal, make sure hands and gears
and even battery are indistinguished
from the bits of thing in the parking lot.

Then take the band and eat it. Without
time, everything becomes Now. And if
you have a compass, break that too. Save
the magnet for ruining credit cards:
There's nothing left to buy. Give
yourself the gift of preservation. Take
a camera and make photographs about
everything you know. Then burn them.

Toss the camera to the sea. What passes,
passes. Eat road signs for dinner. No
one needs to know where you are.

If your phone is still alive and I have
to tell you what to do — Here's This:
leave it plugged and dangle it
out the highest window left. Go
to the pavement, get ladder if need
be, make your last call to Mother,
unless she's dead, then don't bother.
Before you goodbye, set the thing
on fire and hope it takes your
house. Then start walking. I hope
you kept your shoes. All is now.
All is here. All is free. All is
you. Sleep better for knowing this.

Making Mistakes

You can tell I'm coming from a mile away,
　　because the violins start to play,
the violins kick in, like someone kicking you when you're down:
Here come the violins!

I am the woman who goes into the cellar at midnight,
　　during a full moon,
without a flashlight, after the scary noises have started,
and I never hear the people shouting: *DON'T DO IT*
DON'T GO IN THERE YOU'RE GOING TO GET
KILLLLLLLLLLED!!!

And lately, people have been mistaking me for someone they know

Lately I can't hear the voices in my own head,
　　much less the voices
other people hear (voices like mine)
maybe I can't tell whether or not I'm speaking
or speaking out loud—
my speakers are blown out (don't)
the volume knob came off, the balance knob came off,
　　I've lost my balance—

And lately, people have been mistaking me for someone they know

Here's the issue: Some people know what they want,
　　and some people
know what they need, and I know 1300 ways a human can die.
And when I was 8, I was reading the *Book of Lists*,
and there among the ten favorite American sexual positions
and the twelve recorded cases of spontaneous human combustion,
it said there was only one cause of death—
　　one cause for every human death—
The Lack of Oxygen to the Brain! And I thought *Wow! Explosions,
decapitations, people who fall into pits of acid or are eaten alive by sharks,
it makes no difference, there was no oxygen getting to those brains and that's
uncanny* so I ran and told my Uncle Jim, who had just dropped out
of Monastery:

Hey! Uncle Jim! Did you know there's only one cause
      for every human death?
And he said, "Yes. Original Sin."

And lately, people have been mistaking me for someone —

You want me to settle in
You want me to settle down
You want me to settle for you
I do not settle. I take the things I need
And lately people have been mistaking me for someone like that:

I don't know, I don't know anyone like that — you know, those
perfect people who cook and jog and do the *New York Times* — not
just the crossword puzzle, but the whole thing, filling in every
white box in their brains with a Number 2 pencil - for easy erasing
- in case you make a mistake, you can forget it. Forget It! Who are
these people? They have jobs, and they go to museums. They have
good jobs, and they play tennis. They have really good jobs, and
they go mountain-biking in Marin every Saturday. These people
have social lives, and their clothes don't wrinkle; they eat chocolate
but they don't crave it; they respect Oliver Stone, but they really
don't like his work; and in the garage is the Painting Studio, the
Wood Shop, the Sewing Room, the Fallout Shelter.

Killing yourself is an art. You can choose from any number of
ways,
but there are always three things you must keep in mind:
How long will it take? You don't want to be found before
      you're done.
What's the Success Rate? You want to die, not become a vegetable.
What's the feasibility? Can you do it? Will it hurt too much?
Will you be able to finish?
Here's a safety tip: Some medicines should be taken on an empty
stomach, some with food. Check the label to see if you should take
the pills with water, or with milk.

Here, have a beer.
Here, have another.
Have a fifth, have a tenth,

have a drink, have a drink, have a drink, have a drink, have a
drink, have a drink,
keep drinking,
you talk to me when you drink.

Lately people have been mistaking me for someone beautiful.

Tell me you're not expecting anything
                          And I'll tell you I'm expecting someone else
Tell me you don't want a relationship
                          And I'll tell you I already have one
Tell me you'll do anything I want
                          And I'll tell you I don't want anything
Tell me it's not about sex
                          And I'll show you how to make it that way
Tell me it's not about love
                          And I'll tell you you're right —

The issue is this: There are girls who like their bodies, and there are
girls who like their minds. There are girls who like putting out, and
then there are girls who will put out. There are girls who'll go home
with you, and there are girls who'll go down on you, and there are
girls who will clean your clock for asking. There are spit girls, swallow
girls, and gargle girls, and some girls are all three, and some girls are
none of the above and there's no way to tell, because if you ask her
to, she won't, or she won't do a good job, or she won't let you kiss
her, or she won't tell, there's no way to tell her, there's no way to tell
her to, there's no nice way to say *Suck my cock!*

And that's the issue:
Lately people have been making mistakes, and that's news,
isn't it?

Mission Poem

When she dreams, she dreams
Of Mission Street, her body a bus (men ride)
Men get on and off, get on and get off.
Her face is as open as a vacant lot,
Walled in and fenced in and empty
Of all but the dirt, garbage sprinkled
In piles soft enough to curl up in—
But for the broken glass.
Her hands make the shape of a styrofoam cup
Reaching for something to fill it.
Her eyes expand into oceans
Oceans the way they look at night
Cold and wet and black and oh,
They don't stop, they just rush in and out
Like the men from the check cashing shop,
Like the men from the barber shop,
Like the men from the bar,
Like the men from the Triple-Dash-X Theatre.
And her mouth, it is something to dance to,
A soft music escaping the dark,
Lips folding and unfolding, teeth seen
(but rarely) as glimmers of hope.
And when she smiles, if she smiles,
You will feel she has snatched a part of you,
You will feel that something is missing,
You will call her a thief, when you call her.
You will marry that mouth in your mind.

I'm Not Easy

You don't even have the guts to walk down the street by yourself:
You can't keep up with me: I type too fast, I talk too fast,
I'm a fast woman. I like a fast car, a fast drunk, a fast ride
into the parts of town your mother is afraid you frequent.
She worries about you being alone,
and she worries about you being worried.
She worries about bills, and gas leaks, and auto accidents.
She worries about earthquakes, and gangs, and The Mob.
And The Mob? They worry about your mother:
The Mom they call her:
keeping her little boy straight no drugs no sex —

and sex is what drives the world:
a set of legs wrapped around an IBM Selectric,
millions of monkeys tapping frantically on the keys! —
the keys to the car you don't own because you're afraid —
afraid to drive afraid to walk afraid to be seen alone
or with the wrong people: people like me people —
the kind of girl who goes to bars by herself,
drinks whiskey, talks trash, and likes a fast ride:
a nice car tuned so the engine, the engine purrs —
purrs like a woman hit in the right spot:
by millions of monkeys tapping furiously on the keys! —
Do you like the way I drive? Do you like the way I drive?
Do you like the way I drive men to drink?

(unless I'm drinking, then I get myself a designated driver)
Do you want me to drive? Do you want me to drive you?

I am not easy, I am difficult.
I just have a strong learning curve,
and you can earn points by wrapping your legs
in gold foil, by wrapping your legs
around the smooth slick of a motor tuned to purr.

You think of your mother,
                    and you think of what your mother might think.
You think of your mother,
                              even though she's dead.

26

You think of your mother,
                    and she can't say anything to you now.
You think of your mother,
                    and how she must have felt with your father.
You think of your mother,
                    and the thought repulses you,
so you keep driving,
                    gunning the engine like a fat chance,
a fast chance to slow dance,
                    a quick change on the shooting range —

and there's one for you: girls and guns,
and the way they shift gears
from hot to cold, cold to hot, when you fire them, when you hit
     that target:
one million monkeys hitting the keys like a telephone (banana).
1-900-FAST-CAR is the number you'd dial.
Wrap your legs around the gearshift and change —
     change —
     change —
     change
     gears —
float. The way a fat woman floats on her back in a lily pond.
Float. The way an engine floats over the road: carried by car,
carried by car, man and machine and a chick with big tits.
You want a fast woman who drives a fast car,
and you want her on the weekends:

A fast ride, a slow ride, a ride that lets you feel the engine like it's
     yours —
The word 'loins' makes you slightly flushed
when she says it with that mouth of hers:
One million monkeys tapping could not make that mouth.
Shakespeare or no Shakespeare,
I can talk faster than you.

Pepper Spray

I turned my head so I wouldn't see the punch.
I ducked behind the fence
so I'd be able to run,
to call 911,
I braced myself for the wet crunch
    of bone hitting bone.

When the "What you lookin at"
and the "you steppin to me"
and the "you want a piece of this"
and the "it's cool, man"
"it's cool, man"
"it's cool, man"
    had passed,
    had passed,
I looked.

I looked to see my man crying,
hands in front of his face
like a movie zombie,
like a movie blind man,
like a man blinded by zombies,

and he was. A non-participant
    in the initial quarrel, which
    consisted of him *not* walking
    with turned eyes
    past a brother choking his *bitch*
    to get the keys to her car.

Girl got away when Brother stepped
    to my man,
Girl got away and a Third had
    a can
    of a spray
    deemed legal
    and safe
    and carried

by the victims,
the desperate,
and the cops.

This young man was neither threatened
nor desperate
when he pulled this
can of pepper spray on a man
who was unarmed
but defending the girl.

"I broke the rules," he said, as I held his hand and led him,
dripping and blind, the dark two-block stretch
to his basement apartment.

"I broke the rule that says, 'Don't step into boy-girl fights.' "

And it burned his eyes
And it burned his nose
And it burned his skin and mine
for three days after.

I washed his keys and the glasses
that had blocked some of the blow.
I held Kleenex near and thanked
whatever gods kept him
from inhaling it.
I felt the guilt of the anti-hero
for not stopping it
and the relief of the sidekick
who can walk the hero home
when the Kryptonite hits.

Sandy, his roommate, panicked and paced and
told tales of addicts and near-mothers
having pepper-spray heart attacks
in handcuffed captivity.

Sprayed in the face for no reason:
the shit is legal,
but not safe.

You carry that can in your fanny pack
    to keep muggers at bay
    (if they don't take it from you first)
You feel safer for knowing
    the cops are armed with
    "a non-gun alternative."
It's organic, but that don't make it good
when any boy with an attitude
    who's not old enough
    or dumb enough
    to pack a gun
Can use that little can
To put the fear in a man
    dumb enough to save
    a woman's life.

"I broke the rules," he said.
"And I paid for it."

The Thinking Problem

I'm tired of being tired all the time,
bored with being bored;
not much to say to people
who want me to say something,
say something, you're so good
at saying something but listen:
talking doesn't change anything,
and neither does thinking.

Thinking about sleep does not make you less sleepy,
and thinking about food does not make you less hungry,
and feeling sorry for those people sleeping on your doorstep
does not give them a place to sleep—
any more than feeling sorry for yourself.

Thinking a lot doesn't pay very well,
and I've been brought up to want things,
like a house and a car and a nice kitchen—
and *Waah!* I don't have them!
But what good would a nice kitchen do me?
Would I really cook better food?
Would I really balance my budget?
Would I save the world with a garlic press?
Would I save my city from collapsing?
Would I prevent cancer and car accidents?
Would I find everyone a place to live?
Would I stop thinking so much
about thinking so much?

Drinking doesn't cure the thinking problem
any more than thinking about drinking cures the drinking problem—
doesn't keep my radar feet from leading me to that trough—
doesn't keep my hands out of my checkbook—
doesn't keep my mouth from the glass— or the straw.
Straws! whoever invented straws was a lush:
just like the cocktail napkin guy, and the free matchbook guy.
Just like the cocktail shaker guy, and the ice cube guy.

31

They were all guys, and they were all lushes,
and here I am thinking about drinking,
a drink not in my hand and why?
Because thinking does not cure hangovers.
Because thinking does not cure loneliness.
Because thinking, contrary to popular belief, does not cure stupidity.
Just because you think more does not make you a better person,
and if thinking about thinking rates you a philosopher,
then pass the sumac, pass the poison arrows,
pass the torch, I'll pass.

In pictures, San Francisco is so clean and beautiful.
In pictures, San Francisco has history.
In pictures, San Francisco almost has weather.
In pictures, San Francisco is almost a city.
It's got city problems and city smells
and city garbage, but garbage, somehow,
Does not show up on film.

Oh, if talking could take the film off your eyes —
Oh, if thinking could take the hunger out of his —
All these men with famished faces, and
take the hunger out of my eyes —
I am a vulture, yes, I want my prey warm,
but not fighting anymore.
We all circle this place at night,
looking for anyone not like ourselves,
looking for someone without a persistent cough,
with a steady job and clean fingernails,
with a happy history and a happy future,
and meanwhile we let the present slip by
we can't wrap it up, can't unwrap it, can't take it home —
because we can't buy it.

I have work to do, and I am procrastinating.
I am thinking about the work I am not doing; I am not doing
anything. I am thinking.
I am thinking about people I don't know.
I am thinking about two teenagers
asleep in bedrolls in front of McDonald's at 7th and Market.

And I am thinking about the man with the pot belly
and the plastic bags in his back pockets.
And I am thinking about the woman
who has been asking me if I know where a shelter is
for the last two and a half years —
hasn't she found it?

Let me think one last thing.
Why should she have found a shelter
when so few of us ever do?

Good Listener

I could take a phone cord and tie you to the driver's seat—
set the car on fire and walk away—your screaming
would sound like your normal voice—I have to learn
to ignore you someday—I have to learn anyway—

You're going to die in your car no matter what I do.
I'm not going to play Darwin to your God:
Everyone is an asshole but you—you rise to the top—
like cream, like water seeking its own level, or like turds in a bowl:
    the kind that won't go down no matter how much you flush.

Do you see yourself reflected in the toilet water?
Do you gaze into your lover's eyes to see yourself?
Brush back that hair while he dreams of kissing you;
drown out his words so you can analyze them:
drown out the world so you can hear yourself think;
drown out the thoughts so you can hear him:
circle—around and around in the bowl—oh water,

your sign is fire—your sign is stop: I see you: I stop
caring about myself to try to fix the world for you.
No one can fix the world, but I show up with my tool kit:
Here I am with my duct tape, what can I do for you?
Nothing? Oh, well, I'm sorry I came.
I'll go home and fix my broken bathtub if you don't need me then.
Oh! Of course I'll stay on so you can drown your boyfriend!
He needs to be drowned—of course, I agree, of course—

(No, I don't have any problems, because I don't have a lover)
(No, not that she asked, don't worry yourself)
(I call her up and say: I need help, and she says: oh, good,
I'm glad you called, guess what happened to me today: some
    asshole almost hit me on the road)
(Again? What's new? What's ever new? Is anything ever new
    over the phone?)

I could strangle you sometimes, but all that would do is pass
the martyr complex from me to you, only you'd get to be dead,

and I'd get to feel guilty—which is already my steady state, and
when did you become rich and pink and beautiful? And what's this
dust all over my clothes? Has it always been there or—
nevermind. Matter can't be created;
it had to come from somewhere; they
just discovered that new brain cells grow in your head your whole
life: You can't win. You spend your life trying to kill yourself
one brain cell at a time,
but you can't beat those averages—you better start
drinking or shooting heroin or hell—if you want to die why not:

Wrap yourself in the American flag and take a walk on High Street—
Wrap yourself in money and jump into a betting pool—
Wrap yourself in the word of God and head for the land of Nod—

And I say no, for the first time since I've met you—
but I don't even say it, I just shake my head—
and since we're on the phone you can't see me—
but that's okay since you never hear me—
you're deaf, I'm dumb, we make a matched set—
shakers: not salt and pepper but dog and dogged—

like brother and sister only both are only children—
and children grow up but neither of us ever do—
we just get less cute or at least I do—
I guess I'll stand by until you say I do—

and when you do—
lose yourself for another,
I'll have to be glad
that the sanctity of marriage is a covenant,
and you can get a therapist while I join a convent—

I won't be alone and there's no telephone: the best of both worlds
and you're not in them—
but for now I'll pick up the phone when it rings,
and I'll be good I'll listen even talk.

Legend in My Own Mind

So I'm sitting here with a coffee cup with grounds in the bottom but it's the last cup and I don't have the energy to go out and get any more—

more coffee, more cigarettes, more tylenol or demerol or xanax or prozac—and I'm chewing on my thumbnail to get the nicotine out it's been five days I've been in here & haven't moved much—

here comes a cockroach!—I named him Eric after my first boyfriend, and if I'm correct it's the same one I tried to kill on the ceiling last week by shooting my staple gun at the little fucker—but I missed and I missed and I missed and now my ceiling has staples chewing out of it like broken teeth like track marks like a bad suture job—

and have you heard about how people have been getting kidnapped on a train or at a ski resort or in a foreign hotel and they wake up with a kidney missing or 3 quarts of blood gone or the one—my favorite—the man goes home with a prostitute and wakes up in a hot tub full of ice and he's staring at a note that says IF YOU CAN READ THIS CALL 911 BEFORE YOU'RE DEAD that's a good one—

reminds me of the scary story in college about locking your door— it's a true story, it happened on my brother's campus at the University of Maryland; it's a true story, it happened on my friend's sister's campus at the University of Iowa; it's a true story, it could happen to you: the girl goes out for the night—it's always a girl—and she comes back because she forgot her keys—they're on the night stand inside the door—she knows right where they are so she doesn't bother turning on the light just reaches in grabs the keys she's gone to her party—she comes back late that night and the roommate is dead!— cut to pieces!—there's blood everywhere!—and written in the roommate's blood on the wall over the bed is "AREN'T YOU GLAD YOU DIDN'T TURN ON THE LIGHT!"

I swear we all locked our doors for weeks after that one but not often enough or maybe it doesn't matter if you lock your door if you're already inside the room and you can't sleep and you can't get out of bed and maybe if you didn't lock your door you might have a better chance of getting out—

this one time, it was my senior year in college and I can personally tell you this is true, it was Labor Day weekend and I was awake at 3 or 4 a.m. almost everyone was gone for the weekend and there I was reading a book in my dorm room and there was this scraping noise on the window and I thought what the hell kind of bird is up this late at night and then the air conditioner in the window—I was on the first floor—the air conditioner *moves*—the fucking blinds are swinging back and forth and here I am (holy shit) and so I grab the cord and pull up prepared for Cthulu and a man runs away from my window— I call the cops and—shit!—they caught him in half an hour in the old Superfresh parking lot with a foot-long butterfly knife in his pants—

and he says to the cops he just wanted to *look* in the window and I didn't know that knives helped your vision any, although they might if you're the one with the knife—and they asked me what I was doing and they asked me what I was wearing and they asked me could they look in my window to see if they could see me if they just happened to be walking by a girls' dorm at 4 a.m. and later at the trial—I went there as a witness; they don't have special boxes for the perpetrated against—I went there and I was so surprised at how *young* he was— and he pled guilty to peeping—not to attempted B&E—but to standing on his tiptoes outside my window—they didn't mention the knife, and I never told the cops that when I went to make sure my door was locked, it wasn't—

I wish that was the only time I had to call the cops I wish I was the only one who ever had a problem I wish I had a goddamn cigarette and here comes this other cockroach!—I named him Roy—that's right, Roy—after the psycho ex-boyfriend who stalked me and xeroxed my diary and told my mother I was snorting crank—this one kind of staggers now I shot at him with Windex and he didn't die I shot at him with hairspray and he didn't die I shot at him with Raid and Fantastic and fucking contact lens solution and he didn't die— but he always runs in circles now and it was me who crippled him— it was me who crippled myself—it was me who drank the last of the coffee I can't blame anyone else—

did you hear the one about the hitchhiker and the claw stuck in the door of the stationwagon? did you hear the one about the deadliest road in the country where everyone falls asleep—it's in New Jersey— did you hear the one about the prison-trek interstate in Oklahoma? there are signs every half mile: DO NOT PICK UP HITCHHIKERS! did you hear the one about the girl—it's always a girl—who sat in her apartment for so long she forgot how to walk? it was her fault it's always her fault—

here comes Sean!—I named him after my last boyfriend—he's got a leg missing now because I taped him to the floor while I was trying to find a shoe to kill him with, but the little fucker got loose and lost a leg in the process and I think I've been awake for twelve days and maybe I should go find some scientists and say yes, I am hallucinating! yes, I am having stomach cramps!—but the kicker is—I mean you always have to remember—at least you have a door to lock; at least you have your fucking health; at least you're still alive—

and you have all your organs.

Smack (1998 Nostalgia Remix)

For S, P, and A, wherever they are

My best friend—a junkie—he's a smack head
dope fiend pill poppin' tab-droppin program alcoholic
who chain smokes—all at 24 years old.

My best friend calls me at 3 a.m. My best friend says,
I want to cop. I don't want to cop. Come out with me.
Come save me.

      Where are you? I say.
My best friend is walking through the projects
at Avenue D. My best friend is pushing me
through the playground on a Big Wheel.

I'm wearing a dress. It's 4 a.m. on Smack Street,
and I'm worried about flashing my underwear
on a toy bike.

      My best friend is walking on the waterfront
under the Brooklyn Bridge, where the fish come in (fresh fresh).
My best friend kicks a beer can out of the way.

"Watch out for those needles," he says.
"Watch out for those needles," I say.

My best friend is talking about leaving. Leaving this city,
leaving this state. The state of narcotics, the state of New York.
My best friend is talking about leaving this life.

"I've got things to live for, but nothing to die for," he says.
"I'm not going anywhere.
I'm going home."

      We walk to the subway. My best friend
says it's raining. I say, Where? He says, Here. Touches my cheek.

My best friend's a junkie.
He tells me not to shoot. Says he'll pray if I do.

My friend says, "This is working."
My friend says, "This is painful."
My friend says, "This is life.

August 1992 & February 1998

Love Has Always Been My Game

What I Did Today

Woke up and the phone rang.
Told them you don't live here.
Went back to bed and kissed you
goodbye. Stared at the ceiling.
Got up again, showered, smoked
cigarettes. Stared at your body
while you slept. Cleaned the bathroom.
Threw away my diaphragm. Ate a little
oatmeal, drank a lot of coffee. Stared
at the tv. It was still off, you were still
out. Took out the trash. Slept.

Collecting Box Tops

He's looking at me   but not at my eyes
This crowded room   has me paralyzed
Across the bodies   piled on the floor
I see nothing.   I don't ask for more.

The last sex I had   was a one night stand.
He got me as wet   as a desert strand.
I wouldn't say I'm desperate.   I'm not really looking.
I'd give you a date   but I don't do my own booking.

I don't hate men.   I don't like them much either.
"Are you gay, straight, or bi?"   My answer is neither.
I wear pearls in the shower like Mrs. June Cleaver.
That's my love life.   Just leave it to beaver.

You can say no to crack   But not to coke
You can stop jerking off   Well—just one more stroke
You say you don't shoot   You say you don't smoke
If life is a play   Then yours is a joke.

    That little bit
    Where the guy gets hit
    In the eye with a shoe?
    That's you.

As you strut and fret your way across the bar
As you get laid in a stranger's car
As you wish on a plane and call it a star
As you switch from Luckies to big cigars

    Someone else   finds the toy you wanted
    in the Cracker Jack box
    Someone else   finds the boy you wanted
    Sent in the box tops
Just one way
to make your play
to have your say

to make today   Worth waking up for.
                       Fucking whore.
                       You call yourself (this)
                       Collect.

What They Leave

When men leave, they take some things with them, and they leave some things behind. They never leave anything useful, or valuable, or romantic. They take the Mozart CD you secretly thought of as yours, even though you didn't buy it. They leave behind a cranky, dying spider plant neither of you claimed nor watered. They leave behind spare keys you don't recognize, a few pieces of candy in wrappers stuck with lint. They leave empty jars in the refrigerator, empty shampoo bottles in the shower, and books on the shelves that are not empty, but which you will never read.

The things they take mostly belong to them, and you say nothing about the things they take, hoping they will leave something. They will leave something like a Depression glass ashtray belonging to their grandmother, and after you're glad you have this one sentimental thing, after you've stopped calling him and hanging up, he will ask for it back, and you will refuse, and he will come to your house demanding other left things you weren't really aware you had. A sweater. You've worn it, but it felt like payment. For what is unclear.

Sometimes they will take something like a love letter from another man, for similarly unclear reasons, but it is something you want, for clear reasons. Sometimes they will take something else that belongs to you, like a book, and refuse to admit it, even though this is a book he has prized on your behalf, in public, for its value and beauty. Sometimes you will hide things. Sometimes you wish he hadn't left because of what he has taken. Some of the things you wish he'd take, he does, some things he doesn't, some things will stay in your house until you move, which will probably be sooner than you'd otherwise expected, and which has nothing to do with the fact that he's left.

To Forget

You mixed up your verbs again.
Always scrambling tenses,
always writing sentences
and dropping the verb, as in,

"I'll be there when you me," or
"I never meant to you."
Maybe you didn't. The largest lie:
the intention not to hurt. That's why

people speak. Your religion preaches
acceptance, and God's will,
and God wills you to apologize a lot.
Mostly I accept. Sometimes I forget

to forgive, abstaining from the handshake
over the pews: "Peace be with you."
"And also with you." The way you'd write it:
"I take out the trash," forgetting the central verb,

to forget. Your sentences are tense, wiry creatures,
and you complain of forgetting the spelling of words
like "necessary," and "essential." You cannot
spell the words you need; there is more irony

found on one of your postcards than in
all of Valencia's thrift shops. The verb
you confused today is a four-letter word
you can spell any number of ways: L-U-V,

you and me, K-I-S-S-I-N-G. When your thesaurus
suggested "love" and "want" and "lust" and "need"
as synonyms, you thought yourself covered,
thought you'd solved your puzzle: how to get the girl

into bed without loving her? Want her. Need her.
Covet her, envy her, use every deadly sin
to keep her in thrall. In check. You're

more of a noun guy—you like food, drugs are okay,
books and rocks and dogs and sex and art
make you happy. People are nouns, but
they verb a lot, and it's hard to keep straight,
I'm sure. I mix things up myself: I thought

I was in a relationship: symbiotic, sympathetic,
synergistic, symbolic, simplistic. Semantics
get you off and get me on a train of thought,
but I forgot my passport; you forgot to pack your verbs.

Psych Study

And when the skies get gloomy,
the night winds whisper to me:
I'm lonesome as I can be.   —A. Block & D. Hecht, as sung by Patsy Cline

I'm babysitting my sister Katy,
age nine. Katy has Gang Betty Barbie
tied up with tinsel, while Texas Whore
Barbie holds her down, and Damp Mermaid
Barbie slaps her in the face with her shimmering tail.

I'm reading an essay from the University of Nevada
at Las Vegas Psychology Department
on the nature of luck. Are certain personality types
predisposed to win or lose? They hired desperate
people to sit this side of the two-way mirror and roll,

roll, roll those dice—it's a crap-shoot, finding people
who are neither bitter nor anxious nor manic
nor depressed nor suicidal nor addicted to anything
but signing up for psych studies in this City of Sin,
City of Winners and Losers and factory workers,

psych students and torch singers, stealers and
wheelers and used car dealers—how
did they find a control group in Las Vegas?
I read about odds and chance, the weight
dice have in gamblers' hands, the hookers
and hustlers who always roll threes.

My sister is holding Snaggle Tooth Barbie
by the hair over a pit of alligators made of Lego.
"Take that!" she cries, and Trailer Park
Barbie punches Ken in the nuts with a crayon.
I'm reading about hearts and spades. I'm taking

my chances to the bank, comparing my neuroses
to the odds reported by UNLV.
Katy looks up from her Kenner carnage,
gazes at me, blinks twice, and asks, "Tarin,
what's the difference between lonely and lonesome?

I pause and chip some slime green paint
from the nail on my ring finger. "Katy,"
I say, "lonely is like walking home
from school alone on the last day, saying
goodbye to the janitor for the summer,

buying some gum on the way home just so
someone will smile at you. Lonely is the last crayon
in the box that's still sharp, the little lost dog
scratching at every door in town, just hoping
someone will let him in. Lonely is the back seat

of the family car when it pulls down Grandma's
driveway to head the four hours home.
Lonely, Katy, you know lonely, lonely
goes away in a few days, with enough
cartoons and ice cream and skinned knees and make

believe friends." I pause. "You have
friends, right?" "Yeah," she says, "but I can't
play with them over the phone." I nod. "Right."
"So what's lonesome then," she says,
with the biggest, brownest eyes of any puppy dog in town.

"Lonesome," I sigh. "You haven't met lonesome yet.
Lonesome is the last radio DJ awake on a 400
mile stretch of Kansas highway, and it's 3 a.m.,
and it's just you and him and Patsy Cline,
who sang out her heart until it gave in and let her
fly away with the angels, but the angels aren't
with you now, it's just you and the DJ and a double
yellow line, and the semis are all parked on the off-ramp
sleeping, and the night is clear but the moon is gone,
and all you want is a cup of coffee, and all you want
is a pillow, and all you want is your sweetheart,
but he's back in Pennsylvania doing God
knows what, sleeping you hope, but you've got
a whole damn country to put between him and you,
and you drive, you drive and you sing to yourself,
you pretend the DJ can hear you talking,

you decide to drive 50 more miles before
you pull over, and all you want is to be asleep
when the sun comes up, and that's all you want,
and you're not lonely, you're not lonely,
because lonely is all about love,
and you know you won't be loved again.

My sister is very quiet.
I'd forgotten her age. I scoop her
up and kiss her cheek and she says,
"But *I* love you, Tarin," and I say, "I know,"
and I point out the window and say,

"Look, Katy. There's the moon."

Phantom Limb

What are you wearing?
What are you hearing?
What are you doing after all this time?
Don't come lurking round my window
without a good reason, dammit:
Don't blame me for your loss of sense,
your loss of something.
Sometimes I don't know
who lost what here:

It's the first question they ask:
Did he break up with you?
Or did you break up with him?
But that isn't nearly as important
as what got broken,
and sometimes that part's hard to figure out.

I'm your fruitless pursuit —
Hey! I make you wonder —
It has to be something —
It's always something —
usually something strange,
something to catch your eye:

Catch it and stick it in a jar full of twigs and leaves —
don't forget to punch airholes in the lid;
things can die that way, you know.
Don't leave it out in the rain
Don't go out without your hat
You'll catch your death of cold —

You'll catch your death
you're cold
numb
and tingly just like nerve damage, Hey!
You're my phantom limb!
Sometimes I swear I can still feel you —
Sometimes I swear you have feelings —

Sometimes I swear out loud without meaning to—
Sometimes I swear there's a meaning to all this—

If something wicked came my way,
I'd buy it a drink—Hey!
What do you say I don't call you anymore? Hey!
what do you say I get over you sometime soon?
invite you over to not come over—

Dear Miss Manners: How do you tell someone
you don't want to be friends
unless he stops dating other women?
Dear Miss Manners: How do you tell someone
you can't give them the time of day
without having to start from scratch?
and if you scratch my back
I'll be really cautious about what comes next.

Sometimes you're sitting on some steps at night
and looking at the stars
and sometimes you don't even have stars,
you're just sitting there looking;
okay—you're just sitting there.

And this hasn't happened to me,
but what if you showed up and said *Hey!*
what are you doing? (and the truth is
I'm just sitting here
but honesty is not the best policy
if you have secrets)

So I say, I'm just thinking,
but you say *What are you thinking about?*
and what I want to say is, Hey!
I'm thinking about the way you used to look in my bed
when we couldn't leave it for days at a time,
when we used to order in food because it was easier
than getting dressed and talking to people.
We didn't even talk to each other,

but that was okay at the time.
(and when we did leave we went to bad restaurants
so we wouldn't see anyone we knew)
And by the way, have you ever had week-long afterglow?
And by the way, why do you always ask me what I'm thinking?
I guess this is as good a time as any to tell you I always lie,
because I'm always thinking about you.
Should I ever ask you the same question,
you always say *Nothing;* I mean,
you don't even bother to make something up for my benefit —
but when did you ever care about long-term benefits?
When did you get that haircut anyway? It looks terrible.

This is what I really want to say:
There aren't any stars to look at
and what are you doing back here?

My phantom limb.
I swear sometimes I can almost feel you there;
I swear sometimes you almost have feelings.

Discount Pulse Rate

Hey, baby. You got a light?
I've got some dark.
I've got some ideas.
I've got some time to kill, and you look like a good hit man.
Did you come here alone?
Do you come here often?
Do you come often?

What's your sign? I'm a yield.
What's your type? I'm a girl.
That makes me: anything in a skirt.
That makes you: anything that moves,
and I know what you want in a woman.
A pulse.
You want a girl who will get you up in the morning;
You need a warm body to make the sun rise a little sooner,
because if another day has to begin,
it might as well start now;
I can make this easy for you.

I have a pulse.
I have a problem.
I have a pornographic memory,
and a penchant for putting penises
in my scrapbook.

I collect people
like postage stamps: Just cut them
out of my life and paste them into my diary.
Come here, little boy.
I will use you up like a box of Kleenex.
I will unwrap you and put you on and take you off and throw you
    away.

I have a pulse.
I have a problem.
Every night, I have dinner for one
and breakfast for two.

It is always night when I do not sleep,
and I do not sleep unless I am alone.

You don't want to leave me alone, do you?
Don't you want to buy me a drink?
Don't you want to walk me home?
It's a big bad world out there, baby,
and it's a big bad world in here.
My grandmother told me to watch out
for women like me.

I have a pulse.
I have a problem.
I take two in the morning.
I take three or four at night.
I take the moon home in my purse and slip it under my tongue,
wake up and spit it out into the ocean,
which boils over and vomits a single star into the sky.
I do not shine brightly unless coddled and cured
with a lipstick and a stiff shot
of fresh-squeezed human being.

You wanna be my coughdrop,
my throat lozenge, my painkiller, my brandy,
my evening star, my morning constitutional?
I will wear you out like cheap shoes.
I will fold you in thirds and mail you to Wednesday.
You'll be origami, a puzzle box, a folding star.
I will christen you my Good Ship Lollipop.
I will show you the light, and then put it out.
I will show you the door, where you'll knock
on my soft opportunities and then dive into a big glass
of hangover. On ice. You want an olive, honey?

I have a pulse.
I have a problem.
I play Scrabble with my feet, which fit on my head
like a tiara. I will unbutton your ribcage
and insert a homing device—you'll come back
to me like a carrier pigeon.

I'm Capistrano, and you will swallow.
I'm dawn, and you'll crack —
open like eggs into my pan.
Sunny-side up? Scrambled? I am over easy.
I am a side order of sloth.
I am the invention of regret,
the intention to forget,
I am a problem.
Get out your pencils and solve me.

Letter

There's not much I want to say that hasn't been said.
For a while I held illusions like pennies in my hand:
No one has felt like this. Today I dropped my pocket
Full of change into a styrofoam cup thrust my way

Down on Mission Street. It's like this: I could spend my life with scissors,
cutting out phrases of praise from book reviews and horoscopes;
I could comb the Bible, *Songs of Innocence, Twelfth Night,*
Mother Goose, Beyond Good and Evil, and send the wisdom I found

in the form of a fruitcake to set on the mantel each year.
I called the psychic hotline; she said, "Forget him," and hung up.
When I walk into the laundromat, mothers cross themselves
and hide their daughters' eyes: Your shadow hovers nearby,

bodiless, like a kite that shouldn't fly on a windless day;
Like a moth that never noticed the lights are out.

"I Love You" Poem

I love you.
I love you, and I want to pocket your money.
I want to pocket your money, and I've hidden your
   car keys.
I've hidden your car keys, and I smell like a bath
   of jasmine.
I smell like a bath of jasmine, and you're going
   to take me dancing.
You're going to take me dancing, and the moon is
   a celebration.
The moon is a celebration, and you make me feel
   like an opera star, who sings one note
   so long and so beautifully that she keeps
   singing it and forgets how much air
   that will take, and she collapses on the stage
   in a big pile of roses.
And I want to pocket your money, and you should
   then buy my compact disc.
I can see your heart, shaped like an exclamation
   point.
What are you exclaiming about? I already know I am
   beautiful.
The trees are telling us stories.
The trees are telling us stories, and we are buttered
   toast.
I like strawberry jam. I like mangoes. I like pajamas.
I like that pair of shoes
   in the window at Nordstrom.
In the window. Let's go window shopping, and then
   you can brush my hair and I'll sing to you
   in this bathtub full of milk, I'll tell you
   little stories about forgotten kingdoms
   and magic castles and secret doorways
   and witches who have forgotten their spells.
They have forgotten their spells, and I love you.
The next time we eat roast beef, don't let me forget
   to buy horseradish.
Inhale while you eat it. It makes your eyes full of your
   nose.

The horses on Assateague Island just run up and down
    all through the night, and the moon is a
    celebration.
Give me a kiss. We'll sell movies.
We'll sell movies, everyone will buy us flowers.
Tomorrow I am going to pocket your money and buy
    a big bunch of irises.
Tomorrow I am going to ride through the town
    square on a big grey elephant
    covered with rubies and lapis.
Tomorrow I am going to catch the wind up in my
    skirts and fly off to Venezuela without eating
    breakfast.
Tomorrow the showman is going to let me tap-dance
    before the monkey act.
Tomorrow we sweep up big, soft piles of sawdust,
    and we lay down in them.
Tomorrow I love you.
My soft arms will indent you like a paragraph.
My quilted fingers will read your body like a rosary.
My tangled mouth will raid you like a refrigerator.
The bottoms of my eyes will swallow you up like
    Jonah and you'll feel warm and dark
    like a bird waking up from an egg.
We will have dancing, we will have a young girl
    playing a harp.
We will let all our friends come over and cook in our
    expensive kitchen.
We will sign all our letters Her Majesty, and you will
    blush and pretend I didn't say anything.
Yesterday will seem like it took place a hundred pages
    ago, in the desert, with all those gypsies
    looking on through thick veils of bright
    purple silk, and the nightingale, covered in
    rubies, will shout to us not to stop.

Thorn

Kiss me, Judas. I dreamed
you were a lion I dreamed of taming.
In my dreams, I am asleep, and wake
to dream another dream, a solid
lake of worlds ending. A carnival
touch, a campus, a sword
swallowed and brought up again.

I wake to wake like some sleep to sleep,
a revival of eyesight, a present
being born. What is left for day
to expect but another night: closure.
Relieve me from my duty; I was born
at twilight and seek it still, hour
upon hour. Stack each 60-minute

lozenge like a vinyl LP. Funny
how something so thin can hold
such weight. I wait for you to rise,
imagining your dreams, watching
your eyes move beneath their lids.
I kiss your eyelids closed when
you are awake, kiss them open

mornings like this. I can't wake
you now. This stack of clocks will
drop to the turntable when the song
is finished playing, and you play it
familiar, like a photo album brought
to table every Christmas. Look here.
I'm five. I was blonde, I'm blonde

again, taking my past from the bottle.
Drink to remember, drink deep.
I dreamed you were a lion, my thorn.
I will sit here while you try to forget
what the day brings. I remember
how to connect dots. Just read the lines.
I'll read your hands, you read my forehead.

We will shudder the light away.
I'll drink you like milk. I'll polish
your spots, and we'll change our pasts.
Oh, we'll diverge in a forest, and I will be
less traveled on. I'll check my bags,
you check your watch, I'll watch you
walk away like I watch you come

to the surface of all this useless meaning:
You're stirring; I'm the mouse. I could
frighten away your fears, but I have black
coffee problems, and you—you have heroin
problems. I'll show you my etchings:
They're right here on my eyelids, which
open and close like swinging doors.

I'm letting you lie, dog. I always have.
Keep chasing cars, and you'll
lose that leg. I've got one up,
have held both in the air like
rabbit ears. How's my reception?
Change the channel, and we'll swim it
until we sink. Can you tread water? Don't tread

on me. Don't eat the lead paint. I've been
chipping all over the floor. Look:
My plaster is exposed, and you
sculpt it away, just chisel everything
off that doesn't look like me. What's
left? What's wrong? What's keeping you
asleep when I'm falling awake

at 30,000 feet? I've got Delilah
tendencies. I will keep you strong
if you keep me handy. I'll let you
kiss me. I say that to all the boys.
When you pluck me from your side,
consider how I got there. Oh.
You must have slept through it.

Analogy

Crawl out of your hat and wait for me—I'm waiting
with the baseball bat. Look at my handwriting—it says I'm a killer,
a killer in manila envelope. Lick me shut. Kiss my tainted lips.
Bruised, brushed like a suede coat. Blue shoes.

Exclaim to me why you're late. Use each letter of the alphabet as a
verb in a sentence that starts with the letter V. Climb a bamboo
pajama tree. Nail the cat into a box. Lock my ears shut. Plug the
fist into the socket. *MOVE!* Clams in a jam jar. Live? Look at the
arrow stuck in my tendon. Look at the brightness stuck in my eyes.
Look at the fieldmouse stuck to my hero. Look at the pavement
stuck to my wrist.

Your eyes are blank. Someone erased—me. You went missing, but
since I swore I'd never call you, no one ever found out. Dig me up.
I'm under your bed; I've been there since you were nine, waiting; I
knew you were the one for me. I've polished my face for you. Isn't
it nice? Look, here comes a butterfly. Catch it in your eyelashes
and it'll never get away.

Look at the girl you wanted. Look how her eyes are missing.
Look how her teeth are shiny and half her face is hungry.
Look at what you ate for dinner last night.
Look how many swollen mouths are left over.
Look at the popcorn hulls. Look at your teeth when you talk.
Look at me when I talk to you, when I'm tied to your floor.
Look at my bus transfer. It has your name on it.
Look how many beans are missing. Read all the letters you want,
it won't change how I feel.
I'll publish the bottoms of your feet. I'll cast a spell
on the both of you: Ex, ex, ex.

Memory is a preservative whose time has come to be banned.
Writing is a derivative of memory and should be regulated
accordingly.
Photographs are a derivative of writing, of wiring, and of
gunpowder.
What's wrong with this picture? I see a man who isn't any fun.

My turn. I turn you over.
My, what a big rock you must have crawled out from under.
I put you back, I step away. My teeth are trailed with slime.
Under me, here's you. Under you, here's a bed.
Under the bed, here's me. I'm waiting.

Which would insult you more? To be loved, or to be understood?

Something about the eyes. What, are they following you?
Do they glint like hammers? Are they quiet, or swollen?
Do they remind you more of raw hamburger? or of vanilla extract?
Turn me on, I'm a lamp. Turn me out, I'm a pocket. Turn me in,
I'm asleep.

What worries you? What carries you?
What do you feel like when you're alone?
When your mouth is full, what's in it?
When your eyes are closed, who's looking at you?
Which is greater? A villain or the setting sun?
Which is smaller? A blindfold or a minaret?
Which is more closely related? Bees and bonnets or milk and boas?
What does the number two mean to you? The number twelve?
What's that noise in the background?
When you hear that voice calling your name, whose voice is it?
Is your mother living, dead, or indifferent? Does this change when
    it rains?
What was the number of that truck?

How many children does it take to get to the center of a Tootsie
Pop? To screw in a lightbulb? To get to the other side?

How normal is normal? How wide is the ocean? How wet water?
How do you get something out of the box if the box has no lid?

What if the box is an apple?

Telephone rings, do you pick it up? Someone is staring at the back
of your head. Do you pick it up? Comic book in the gutter. Do you
pick it up?

Something about the goddamn eyes, did you write it down,
did you write it down? All across town, you didn't write it down.
All across the bay, you smiled and ran away.

Tip it over, see what comes out. A spout, full of worms, tip it over.
Bring me a drink, fill it with ruby ice. Eyes. Ice cubes. Same thing.
You're my ex-brother. You're the man I used to be a woman with.
You're the drum I used to beat. You're the man I used. To be a
woman. With your drum. I used the beat.

We used to say digital and analog. We used to be analogous.
We used. An analogy: You are to me as water is to empty. You are
to me as road sign is to car. You are to me as road sign is to Las
Vegas. You are to me as Los Angeles is to leave. You are to me as a
life is to lead. You are to me as dark is to darker. You are to me as
nine is to nine. You are to me as division to subtraction. As a bell is
to ring. As 1949 is to 1065. You are to me as my mother to your
father. As Freud to a flame. As monkeys to bars. You are to me as
deep is to drink. You are to me as deaf is to blind. You are to me as
frog is to jump, as wine is to water, as wealth is to death. You are to
me as hole is to head.

Something about oblivion. About the way people see each other. Something about not thinking. Clarity of thought, Mamet character wanting to achieve complete purity of thought, meaning no thought, just being, like animals or people who are slow. Achievement of such. Surprise at envying those I despised and scorned. Something about friendship. Story about men and women falling in love. My story. Something with a car, a drive in the night that as far as I know has not happened. Maybe a convertible. Maybe leaning seats back, looking at the stars, but looking at him, and he's looking back. Face near the gearshift. His face. Maybe he's in the backseat looking up from behind the driver's seat. Maybe I'm leaning back in my seat, still belted in, waiting to see what he's going to do. He's going to kiss me.

Thoughts about Justice and God. Something about Lucifer, angel of light. About casting off those who most loved you. About being God, and determining what justice is. About people who do this every day. About him, his way of judging your contours, weighing in favorable. Judging how you feel on the inside. Judging himself by whether you come. Grasping your hips. Slapping you lightly, your hips, your thighs. Whispering into you. Kissing your darkness, making love to it with the same mouth he uses to judge you. He judges you by kissing you. He judges you when you come. He does not announce his verdict. Every time he decides something about you, he files it away, later making large wall-charts of pros, cons, and things to watch for. Sometimes you can tell. Sometimes his eyes light up when you do something he would have loved for you to do. These are both pros and warning signs. Warnings that you're learning too quickly what he is like, and what he could want from you if he'd let himself own you. He knows he could have you. And he's not taking you. "This is fair," he tells himself. He has power and is not taking it. He is suffering for his decision by denying himself gifts he has been tempted with. You are suffering from his decision by offering yourself and being borrowed.

Perhaps he is not God. Perhaps he is afraid of rejection. Perhaps he wants to dance on the abyss. And then, perhaps, he doesn't know where the abyss is. Something, a movie, with those god-with-a-small-g conversations, maybe your life in coffeeshops and diners. Characters simple and very smart, very odd, they always think of those snappy retorts now, not two hours later, like that conversation by the pool. Your life as a screenplay. The author has a strong sense of irony. Everything fits together. There are no loopholes. Perhaps he wants a loophole.

Yes, I came. I came enough for me, so shut up.

2-point Conversation

Here we are again, sitting across
this table. You are cradling some dice now
in those same slightly burnt fingers; I am
sucking on ice, and which one of us
is thinking about dicks? My eyes are
swollen again, and you ask me if I've been
crying. Of course. Over me. Of course not.

It's been about three years since we sat here,
and last time it was just as shitty, you
and me at odds like the world trying to
take on Sony. You roll some dice. Three,
five, three. All dice have chance
built in like an airbag. You're never sure.

No one cares if you're crying over me or
over anything else—you don't make a big
enough deal out of your dramas. Little things
interest you. You belong to the Queen of
Clubs. I'm sorry.

Dreary night. An epic dreary night.
The night you thought to light
your hair on fire was just like this.
Cold blue steel gun gray. Not a bit
of fuzz to it tonight. Dreary,
unforgivable, unfortunate. Trash
can lids clattering in the alley
below. *Meow. Bang. Meow.*

Take your wings out of the freezer.
Open the package. Scotch-taped
bitches. I don't take no chicks
from ditches, no bitches left
in standing water. Brillo pads scrubbing
the surface of your eyes. Begging
some sour forgiveness. Lemon drops
raining from the sky. Your tongue

coated in rage. Salvation Army Corpse.
Here we are, immaculate and driven,
driven to some sweet victory
over the hand-soap companies.
It's all been said before, probably
better, but oh, yes, we go on
talking anyway, don't we. Forget
everything. I used to know you.

Piles of rubber bands. Navy blue
handset to a hot pink phone. Stop
touching your hair like that. You're
like every other woman. You gots tits
and you think it makes you special.
I'll give you today's special. I'll
give you your soup-of-the-day.

He always wants a refill. He always tips
in dimes. Shadowy legs climbing up
the chimney, spidery whispers just
behind your ear, don't touch —

Justice has its hold on you, and
justice has its smell. Newly
varnished creamy tabletop checkered
foil — let's make some calls and
have some sex in this pile of hair.
I don't know whose hair it is.

Oh, precious, deliver me from evil,
the evil fingertips. Cut it out, you'll
break it.

They don't know how to crowd as well
as they used to, do they, darling? I've
been having dreams of drowning and
now everything is just as blue —

Afterwards

Here we are: I can't believe it's afterwards already. I know there are words, somewhere, but they're locked up, in the velvet-lined box in that glass-doored cabinet my grandmother kept full of Depression glass.

The bottom drawer held a stack of letters tied with twine. I always guessed they were love letters, and the words I need are in the middle of that stack. The seal on the back is broken, a little wax medallion hovering in wait.

The colon between the numbers radiating red from my alarm clock beats on and off and I swear I can hear it, like a heart, one-two, one-two, one-two, as I lie on the floor, barely brushing your side with my leg, like a twig

on a pane of glass. I am shining on the floor like a window lit by the moon. I am cradled by a cushion of heat built up from somewhere. I couldn't speak my own name if I had to. I think I'm made of tea and cinnamon, clover

honey and ginger, birch beer and whipped cream. I 'd melt if I knew how. Morning. I don't remember sleeping. I don't remember waking. I don't remember the divisions between days, or the sound of the telephone.

It's not the falling part of love that trips me up. It's the landing. The engine failure, the plummeting, landing gear stuck inside, and we left the parachutes on the runway back in Uruguay. It's time to wait.

Time to do the Tennessee twelve-step: I accept that there is a power greater than myself. And that I'm in bed with him. I can't believe it's afterwards already. Morning means getting out of bed, and the idea feels bristly,

like ripping a band-aid from your knee. It's time to wait.
Pretend there's company coming over, get out the good dishes, the plates that look lime-flavored, the teacups rimmed with little globes as smooth as peeled grapes.

Pretend that nothing's wrong, pretend there's nothing odd about making coffee for two and scrambling eggs. Pretend you always make orange juice. Pretend that mornings have nothing to frighten you with. Pretend

you're not alone.

Shallow Water
No Diving

Sonnet

This is the first line of the poem.
The second line is better.
By the time you reach the third line, you wonder
what will happen. What the point is. What the fourth
line, or the fifth will say, if anything. How often do you
count to six, using fingers? Using dice? The next line
uses a device called a caesura. Say seven. Say anything
that starts with the letter eight. Count out loud. Count
on me. Count on this line to use the number nine.
Are we waiting? Tense, Tent, Tennis, Tendril, Ten.
This old man, he played eleven, shot his dog and went
to twelve. "Indians" or "niggers," it's still Agatha Christie.
Thirteen. Elevator stop. The floor beneath
fourteen. The sky above the last line in the poem.

Epitaph

Since you have spent more hours
or days staring into your glass
than you will ever spend
looking in my eyes;

And since one stiff drink can
hold me all night long
the way you never could;

It's clear that I should stick with Jack,
and you should stick with Jim,
and then both of us will be happy.

"I love you," he says.

"Stop saying that!" I shout.

"But it's true," he says, and goes back to murmuring.

I am almost frustrated enough to leave, but I know I'd have problems finding my clothes, finding my glasses, finding the light switch in the first place. I have never had to keep telling a man to stop it, stop saying you love me, and I don't speak the truth we both know: We have known each other a little more than forty minutes, and even if, *even if* I believed in love at first sight, this would hardly be it.

We've spent twenty of the last forty minutes trying to coax his marinated cock into performing the bestial act we came to his apartment for in the first place. The reason we met, you could say.

"If this dick was a person, it couldn't drive," I think. I suppress a giggle. This dick *is* a person, and he's luckily carless. Carless, careless, nearsighted, and possibly middle-aged, although I can't tell in this light. Not someone I'd have normally picked out for a romp on the futon, but I was two or three bourbons past caring.

When they were walking me home—him and his ex-girlfriend— oh yes, I was confused too, the two of them were walking me home, me wondering *how ex is she?*, me wondering *both of them?*, me wondering why I had that last drink in the first place—when they were walking me home, I was thinking already: At least it isn't far to my apartment from here.

I am barely conscious, and he's managed to put a condom on his miniature penis, coaxing it to attention just long enough to put the rubber on, at which point it rolls over and plays dead.

Already I am thinking of my plan of attack if I run into him in the bar again after all of this is over.

"His *fingers* are bigger than that," I think, and I fall asleep while he does it over and over again: *Stroke, Stroke, Attempt, Fail! Stroke, Stroke, Attempt, Fail! Stroke, Stroke, Attempt, Fail!* I'm failing, I'm falling asleep, I'm grimacing to myself as he says, "Oh, baby. Oh, I love you," and again sinks his head between my unconscious knees. May as well be frostbitten. May as well be drowned.

"Oh, fuck me," I say, halfheartedly.

I wake up sometime close to dawn and the whole charade begins again until I realize that it's futile, it's worse than futile, it's impossible,

I find my glasses, I find my clothes, he wants a kiss, he's not bad at that, I walk naked to the bathroom, ignoring roommate noises, I get dressed.

"I love you," he says.

"You're impossible," I say, and as I'm tying my shoes I ask him, "What was your name again?"

Abecedarian: Ask Bobby

Ask
Bobby to
Come over and
Drink. We've got
Enough booze
For us and him too.
Granted, it's not
High quality stuff.
It's rotgut, but it's
Just booze with no gimmicks.
Kills your
Liver, but then,
Most stuff does.
Now that I'm getting
Older I think
Perhaps of
Quitting. Not to say
Risking brain cells isn't
Satisfying. Being
Temperate has all the appeal of
Ugly shoes on a fat girl.
Vats of creamed liver.
Washing strangers' toilets.
Xperts advise moderation.
You advise drunkenness.
Zero ventured, zero gained.

Oral Fixation

I have spent my whole life
putting things in my mouth.

It always starts with nipples
(thumbs toes pennies people).

My mother's secret sleep potion:
one small McDonald's fries.

Put the girl in the back with the food
and she'll chew herself to sleep.

Mornings I'd stand up in my crib
to watch the trains, the rain, the squirrels

on the roof. I practiced taking things
out of my mouth. Small dogs, birds,

the sky, the light, the universe. "Where
do you live?" A favorite party trick at three.

"I live in the Towers house. In Grantsville,
in Garrett County, in Maryland,

in the United States of America,
in North America, on the planet Earth,

in our solar system, in the Milky Way,
in the whole universe. My zip code

is 21536. I live right here."
These were things I took

from my mouth and used to tack
the world in place. If my crayons

melted, I cried. I was stung by
a wasp. Don't tell me about pain.

I am not a nail biter, but thumbs
led to pencils, pencils to pens,

pens to candy, gum, cigarettes. Like chewing
on the end of your life. Like using

your mouth as a blow torch, breathing fire
to prove you can still breathe at all.

I wake to brush my teeth
and I brush my teeth to sleep.

If I could chew on Alaska, I would.
If I could chew on Italy, I would.

My sister ate my homework once.
An hour's worth of algebra. She was

reaching for the textbook when I
caught her. She gazed at me, three,

and asked me why there were
so many stars in the sky.

Picky

By the time I learned
I could rule out gay men
I'd decided I could be picky.

No more boys with bad hair,
and bad teeth were out.
I could reconsider casting

spells on the short. I have
never liked dumb guys,
but I never disqualified them.

One day I decided I'd take
my time alone instead of waiting,
wasting my time on men I found

unappetizing, unappealing,
unclean. I have made rules
for my menu selections.

Is it too much to ask
that a man have a job?
Or a phone? Or a bath?

"Never date anyone
crazier than you" is a standby
I too often forget. No more alcoholics, no more

drug addicts, no more foot fetishists.
No droolers. No colostomy bags.
Boyfriends should never

out-accessorize their girlfriends.
No purses. No guns. One felony
per customer, please. The line

between kinky and catheter
is not a thin one. He should
love his mother, but not

too much. If he brings condoms,
he's smart. If he brings a condom
case, he's history. If he brings

his toothbrush on the first date,
he's a bit too smug. I hate smug.
But he must brush his teeth.

If he has hair, he should brush
that, too. And I'm going to make a rule
about that guy's hat.

Walter

"Walter," she said, "I'm leaving you."
"Honey?" he said. "Can you get me another beer before you go?
"I mean, since you're up?"

How To Break Up With Your Boyfriend

1.

Let me begin with reassurances
that no relationship was harmed
in the making of this poem.

Every boyfriend I've had,
real or imaginary,
had a solid chalk outline
before my pen touched this paper.

Breaking up, after all,
is a singular skill,
like juggling, or glass-blowing,
or swallowing fire.

2.

Call out another man's name,
not just in bed, but in the bathroom.

Tell him you found lipstick on
his collar. And if he's innocent, refuse
to believe him. If he asks for evidence,
burn his shirts.

Post the numbers for U-Haul,
Goodwill, and Roto-Rooter on the fridge —
just in case.

Call up his mom
and tell her what he's like
in bed.

Take to listening to
Metal Machine Music.
On repeat. While going to sleep.
Tell him it scares away the monsters

under his bed.
Set the table for three,
and tell him you're not expecting
anything.

You could let it end
like a game of Monopoly:
After a while, everyone gets bored
and goes home.

3.
When confronted, tell him nothing's wrong.
Tell him you just want to make sure
that you can live without him.

Punk Rock Boy

for the guys at the Horseshoe

I just got stoned, and I'm fresh out of Cheetos
My mom is all worried about AIDS from mosquitos
The car is in drive, but my mind is in neutral
I compliment the dog when the girl is what's beautiful

My roommate's dealing acid out of the freezer
My back is all hairy and I can't find the tweezers
Spent my last ten dollars on a two dollar whore
The sign says pull, but you have to push the door

I gotta get some money to buy a tattoo
The bread is for me and the crust is for you
I hitchhiked here with a two dollar bill
Lost my new leather jacket at the Bottom of the Hill

Punk rock is dead, and crystal is clean
I'll even dance to disco if it gets me on the scene
Met a green-haired girl with a cornbred heart
She gave me her number, but I lost it on BART

My degree is in physics, and my planet is Venus
But I work in a coffeeshop and talk about my penis
My taillight went out, so I had to sell the car
I'm nineteen years old but I get into bars

I met this girl on AOL
Her voice is from heaven and her body's from hell
I should go to the clinic and see if I'm sick
Or else I'll stay home and play with my dick ring

Next week, man, I'm going to clean up my act
I'm gonna get a job and I'll stop shooting smack
I won't be running my mouth anymore
The sign says pull, but you have to push the door

Judas Was a Girl

Lips like a clown
frozen into hamburger-biting posture —
gifted with rubber lips,
she sneers when she bites,
and she bites when she talks,
and she talks about God
like she's met Him.

"Yeah, I was having a beer with Jesus the other night,
and He said they don't make wine like they used to,"
or like He used to, I guess.

I can see her now, toasting the Holy Spirit,
buttering Him up,
using her knife of a mouth
to kiss those wounds and make Him cry, and
"Jesus wept," she said.
"It was fuckin' rad."

Abridged Virgin

"If that's all there is, my friends, then let's keep dancing." —J. Lieber

I was tired of being a virgin. More than that, I was tired of being an abridged virgin. All those cocks and no pussy. Not my pussy, anyway.

Picking guys up at parties was easy. All you had to do was show up around the time the keg was running out and smile at a guy. If picking up guys was easy, getting rid of them was even easier. If you only gave him a handjob, there's no way he'd try to stay overnight. I was the queen of handjobs.

My freshman year in college, I had been satisfied with the sort of manual dexterity guys get from playing a lot of arcade games. I could get multiple orgasms from finger fucking, and who can really ask for more than multiple orgasms?

Okay, love, affection, tenderness, cuddling—you don't get any of those from picking a guy up at a party and giving him a handjob. But the reason I had held out for so long was that I couldn't in good conscience imagine looking back on my life and remembering *this* drunken slob as the guy I'd first put out for. And I didn't want to sleep with someone I actually liked, because I'd probably end up falling in love with him, and that had never been a pleasant experience in the past.

I'd held out on my high school boyfriend, Eric, who was the child of carnies who were in town for the winter and moved back and forth to Florida with the carnival season. I moved on to hold out on two other guys who also moved to Florida. I didn't put out for Charlie, Jeff, Brian, Jimmy, Seth, or Brian's little brother, even though we were all half-naked and drunk on Mad Dog in the attic of my parents house while they were on vacation. I ended up in bed with Jeff at another party, the other guys listening outside the door as he begged, "Come on, I've already got the condom on." I took a bath with Jeff's best friend, Charlie, and I didn't fuck him. Charlie slept in my bed several times and I still didn't fuck him.

The pattern thus established, I went to college, and successfully avoided sleeping with Jake, Devin, Toby, Phil, Jamie, and another Jeff. I went to bed with and didn't screw Matt, another Matt, Peter, some guy named Colin's brother whose name I don't know, a Dave, an Archer, a Philippe, and yet another Jeff, this last one on the baseball diamond in the middle of October. I also didn't sleep with an

Englishman whose girlfriend lived across the hall, although she heard so much noise coming from my room that she asked me what kind of action I got last night. I swear I didn't know he was dating Darby. I swear.

By the time I hadn't slept with Judas, I knew it was time to do something drastic.

I had a crush on a guy who lived in town, an alumni named Scott Karr whose nickname was Race. Race Karr, get it? He was awfully pretty and awfully short and I decided that I was going to seduce him and get it over with once and for all. I had my reasons. He was planning on moving out of town.

I went downtown to Scott's house and Scott wasn't home, but his roommate Steve and a couple other guys were just sitting down to watch a movie and asked me if I wanted to join them. I said sure. The movie was *Eraserhead*. I had never seen it before. In case you haven't seen *Eraserhead*, let me summarize the parts I remember for you (all inaccuracies are irrelevant):

> There's this guy who's terrified of everything, but particularly women. His hobbies include watching the lightbulbs burn, listening to the radiator, fantasizing about strange women, and not sleeping. So he gets a girlfriend. Her mother is a monster who asks him if he had sexual intercourse with her daughter. He dreams or has visions of wormlike, spermlike creatures that infest everything. He gets his girl pregnant and she gives birth to a monster—this time, a bonafide monster. So he has to get married. And then things get worse.

I went back to campus and knocked on the door of the guy who lived across the hall. His name was Lowell Slouch. He was a notorious slut, drinker, and pot smoker, in increasing order of magnitude. He was cute. He had a southern accent. He'd do fine.

A few months earlier I'd pulled this cute little girl stunt where I knocked on his door and asked if I could borrow some CDs, because I'd just bought a CD player and had nothing to use it on. He'd gotten me wasted and held my hair while I puked in the cold bathroom. At the time, we all thought it was funny that I'd gotten so drunk on one gin and tonic. Years later, I realized that the single gin and tonic was about 16 ounces of gin to one ounce of tonic over ice in a 20-ounce glass.

I knocked on his door and asked if I could come in.

Ten minutes later, we were making out. The album was Led Zeppelin II.

He pulled back and gazed deep into my eyes. "You wanna get crazy?" he said. Yes, he actually said that.

Yes.

"Are you sure?" The date rape witch hunt went into full swing that year and guys were trained to ask once and then ask a second time if the girl was sure she wanted to have sex so that everyone was on the same page about it.

Yes.

His dorm room was done in Neo-Harem Love Den style. He'd surrounded the posts on the bunk bed with tapestry-print cotton sheets so that you had to climb into the bed as if through curtains.

And so there I was having sex! Or rather, I was about to. He was putting on the equipment. I was trying not to act afraid. Not of sex. Of his incredibly enormous cock. I had handled approximately nineteen penises in my nineteen years, and this was by far the largest I had ever seen. It was as big around as my wrist and as long as a Harlequin romance novel. In fact, it was about the same size as the American Heritage Dictionary paperback edition, only of course it wasn't as wide.

"Well," I thought, "it's supposed to hurt." I started doing my deep breathing exercises that I'd perfected for my visits to the gynecologist.

On the other hand, the gynecologist warns you.

"So, is it big enough for you?" Yes, that's what he said.

"Um, excuse me?"

"Ahem, um, I mean, are you enjoying yourself?"

Trying not to keep from laughing.

Ten minutes later neither of us had come and I was confessing.

"Oh. Well, I kind of wondered why your initial reaction was so strong." (His exact words, ladies and gentlemen.)

"Um, yeah."

"Well, what do you think?"

"Well, all I can think is, 'Is that all it is?' "

He laughed a good laugh. "Yep. That's all it is." Guys seem kind of skittish about virgins, but he got a good kick out of learning me the ropes—I didn't tell him what I had or hadn't done already, and he didn't ask.

So we fucked around for a while longer, a little of this and that, and yep, that's all there was to it. Anti-climactic doesn't just mean

91

that I didn't have an orgasm—that I expected, from years of reading *Seventeen* magazine. Anti-climactic means that after all the scheming I'd done, that sex wasn't much more than an internal handjob.

And then. And then. And then he decided it was time to smoke a cigarette. He ignored my snide comment about the cliché of smoking afterwards, because it was just beginning to dawn on him that there was too much sticky wet for what we'd actually accomplished. He dragged me into the fluorescent-lit bathroom and Dear Jesus it looked like we'd sacrificed a virgin in the sense of slitting her throat and eating her beating heart. We were covered in more blood than I'd ever seen in one place. And it wasn't just the blood that was disturbing—it was the perfect handprints of blood covering both of our backs.

We started giggling. It was as if the Arthur Murray Dance Studio had branched off into instructional sex videos, sticking handprint stickers here and there on models' bodies to show you where to put your hands. Years later, I smirk to myself and think that bleeding is probably the only way to guarantee the guy will change his sheets between girls.

We washed up a little, smoked our cigarettes, and made promises we didn't mean about how having sex with your friends is the best way to go. He compared sex to smoking a joint, said that it's more fun to share than it is to do alone. "I get you high, you get me high." We told each other lies about staying friends and doing this again sometime. We took our showers separately and slept in our own beds. About a year later I heard that he was engaged in this incredibly reprehensible contest with another guy about who could shag the most girls: a point for every different girl, and virgins were worth three.

A little while after that I heard he dropped out of college.

He wasn't much better than the drunken losers I'd conscientiously avoided sleeping with, but I can say with confidence that I got a better story out of him. I still count the experience as "good sex," because I was certainly engaged in it the entire time.

I no longer consider intercourse to be one step above fingerfucking, and I still have multiple orgasms.

Friedrich Nietzsche came to me in a dream and told me the law of supply and demand is a myth. Eyes, flicker like candles, turn towards the lane. Picking them up like blackberries, eating them, sucking the seeds. Everyone warned me, and I never claimed they didn't. Groaning in the sky with the hangover of the day's events lying curled in our shadows. We are not awake yet.

We carry a small mirror with us everywhere so we can check and make sure we're still breathing. When we wake up in the morning, we cast shadows, first thing. We know how and where to use apostrophes. We color only outside the lines, baby, the part no one but us can see. Shining, ducking, giving lessons in the art of dissonance and warmth. A small token.

Window somewhere, someone's rapping on it. I dare you let him in, I dare you check and see his knuckles are bone. Soft spill of marbles onto the floor. Slow sweep of a very large gun. Vibration of the sink as the water drips into it. *Careful, she's armed.* You must tell them what you want, and within thirty seconds, you must have them hooked. Keep them in order by number.

You all have assigned seats. It's partially so I can learn your names. It's partially to torture you by permanently situating you between two people you hate but who themselves get along famously. There's some poor kid, 23, 24, sitting in the SAT's wondering how to begin the test if you can never open the booklet. Someone skipped part A-16. *All of this is in lowercase, this next*

part. Deadpan. Pokerface. Slackjawed. Wideeyed. You've derailed my train of concentration camps. Franchise wigs. Let your fingers do the caulking. I've been carrying around this guy's bowling ball for a really long time just hoping he'll show up. Don't forget to rinse off the pickles before you eat them. She's toiletry-trained. Issues of defenestration. Skywriting. Closet hooks. Dawn.

Three Observations on Belief

She believed she was cursed. She believed her guardian angel had been detained at a flea market by someone selling tarnished halos. Her halo was not tarnished. Kahlua's halo was spun from the finest fiberglass and no one else could see it, but no one else had ever looked for it, she figured. She believed she was cursed, and she knew you were following her.

The boy's father found it easier to make schemes about selling disaster than selling talent. "If you had a horrible skin disease," he said, "We could make so much money. We could walk around saying we were too poor to take care of your awful skin disease, your terrible skin disease, and people would give us money to fix it. We would keep the money, and your skin would get worse. They'd give us more money, and I'd say, 'I've bought everything.' And they'd develop a cure. And when we were really rich, and no one knew about it, they'd cure you, and we'd move to another country."

I could have believed that your girlfriend died. I could have believed you were on the rebound. I could have believed you got even more depressed when I fell in love with someone else. I could have believed you failed a class because of me. I could have believed you slept on a couch in a trailer park. I could have believed you smoked crack. I could have believed you got over me that quickly. But when you did, I didn't believe you at all. Not at all.

Dumps

So what is it, what's the matter, what's got you down?
Your girlfriend left you? Your dog died, someone stole your
secret chili recipe?
You got fired, evicted, dumped, trumped, snubbed, rubbed
the wrong way?

You're looking down in the dumps, pal, and I know from dumps.
You're long in the face, got the blues, sourpuss, party pooper,
Raining on my parade like that!
In every life a little rain must fall—
Give up, give in, give out, give me a nickel, got the time, got a
cigarette
Got
Got
Got
Got
Got
Got a problem?

HEY YOU! WHAT'S YOUR PROBLEM?

Do you have a small dick? A big ass? No breasts? Breasts too
large?
You can't lift anything bigger than your head? Your arms are
flabby?
Your back aches, your watch stopped, your neck is too thick,
your toes are ugly? You have cellulite? Corns? Bunions? Warts?
You have too much hair? Not enough? Your nose is the wrong
shape,
 your eyes are too close together, you don't have a chin?

You weren't abused as a child, but you wish you had been,
so you'd have a reason to be such a fuck up? You don't get laid?
You get laid often enough but it's always eerily unsatisfying?
You can't hold a steady job? You have a steady job but it's
meaningless?
You have a meaningful job
you should love but it just isn't what you want?

You've never been away from your home town?
You've never had a home town?

Maybe you should string Christmas lights from your tits and hire a
good marching band.
Maybe you should ask before you take one.
Maybe you should take two and call me in the morning.
Maybe you should wake up *before* you go to work.

Write yourself a note to remember to throw away the notes you
don't need anymore.
Put all the extra stuff in a box marked "Extra Stuff."
Label each bookshelf "books."
Arrange your shirts by color, your socks by mate, and your towels
    by age.
Don't forget to clean the phone. Brush and floss twice a day.

Maybe you should wash behind your ears.
Maybe you should spread the Good News.
Maybe you should spread it a little thicker.

You can't flex muscles you don't have.   (Take out the trash.)
You can't buy happiness if you don't have money. (Take out the trash.)
Nothing beats a good blowjob.   (Take out the trash.)
You can't boil anything alive—not the whole time you're boiling it.
                                                (Take out the trash.)

Maybe you should break it if you buy it.
Maybe you should like it if you try it.
Maybe you should kiss your mom good night.
Maybe you should hold your lover tight.
Maybe you should quit before you start.
Maybe you should break your lover's heart.
Maybe you should ask the girl to dance.
Maybe you should wear the pants/that fit you.

Maybe it's time, maybe it's time   to wake up
                                        to get up
                                        to go out
                                        to quit drinking so much

to quit thinking so much
to quit sinking yourself

into those holes you keep digging.

Let's quit quitting.
Let's start something.

Bus Transfer Poem #3

Unlike men, bus transfers come with a warning:
VOID IF DETACHED.

Had you come with a warning, I never would have gotten on;
Had you come with a warning, I never would have come at all.

We Apologize for Any Convenience

Samantha

Samantha decided she needed a pseudonym, so she called herself Charlotte Explodes. She submitted a manuscript to a small but excellent college that was rather expensive and that promised to give her a scholarship if she attended. Samantha went for a visit to this college with all the other contenders for the scholarship; she was aware that she was the best writer of all the possible high-schoolers interested in attending this small, but excellent college in the middle of nowhere.

Samantha's manuscript was included in a chapbook of all the submissions of all the high school students attending that special weekend at that small—but excellent!—college on a slyly pretty campus. It was a tradition among the upperclassmen, the various Holden Caulfiends at this small, slyly excellent college, to peruse this chapbook of high school girls and boys and make fun of what they found there.

They found small, poorly written poems and stories from small, but excellent high school students. It was what they always found. The exception was a story or poem by Charlotte Explodes. The writing wasn't bad, they all concurred; although none of them could remember much about it, they all concurred. What they did remark on was the name: Charlotte Explodes! And her book was to be called "All Over the Ceiling." They all concurred. Small, but excellent (the joke).

Small, but excellent: the girl, the party, the boy she followed home, the ensuing fight and embarrassment. Charlotte Explodes, all right, said one very fat girl. Charlotte gets drunk and Explodes, Everywhere. Small, but excellent. The college. Charlotte was Samantha was very embarrassed to be in the next room when the Colden Haulfields began their snickers and sly, petty remarks about the evening before. Charlotte vowed she'd show them all. Samantha accepted their small, but excellent scholarship. Pretty sly.

Junk Drawer

I am the woman in front of you in line who digs for her wallet in a bag larger than a small dog, and then stands in the doorway, putting away her change. She has gloves, an umbrella, a magazine, and a receipt for everything

she's ever bought. She has phone numbers in case of emergency. She's filled out that card in her wallet that specifies who to contact in the event of her untimely death. She has a datebook (full), a wallet (empty), and a spoon—

just in case. I can't find anything. I need a head-based pegboard. What I have is a corkboard coated in news from last year: lists of things to do (with half the items left unchecked), pictures of children who've grown up, and clippings

that are no longer relevant. Cartoons made obsolete by design. Warranties for long-dead appliances. Instructions on how to operate machines that have been sold. Phone numbers of friends who have moved. A birthdate with no

name specified. Boxes for things I'd never admit to owning. Reminders to call the bank, the plumber, Mom and the dentist. Postcards from everyone: "What are you up to these days? I heard you moved. Write soon."

I have a set of alphabet magnets in my head: never enough vowels to say what I want. I'm playing Scrabble with ZQXFMGI on my plate. I spell FIG and hope for a U. I get W. I could have spelled GYMNAST two turns ago. I am lost.

I'm like fly paper, everything sticks. I'm like a lint trap no one cleans out. When I walk down the street, verbiage sticks to me like toilet paper stuck to the bottom of a model's shoe. I come home coated in old news.

Every time I get a haircut, fools rush in. I can't wear earrings anymore, because it makes my head too heavy, what with all the scrap metal and spare parts I'm carting around. I don't want a better mousetrap, because then

I'd have to throw away the one I already have. I can't read the mail, or then I'd have to answer it. I can't meet anyone, or else I'll have to remember their names. I can't do anything, because then I'll have to find something else

to worry about. My laundry does itself. My books read themselves. My stomach eats itself. My friends talk to themselves. They all think I'm listening, but I can't hear them: There's too much in the way.

For the Birds

You can't understand me unless you speak my secret code,
and you can't. Therefore, you don't know
what I mean when I mean what I say,
if I say anything at all. For example,
every word in this poem means something—

possibly what's in the dictionary; maybe not.
I'm not into synonyms and antonyms.
I've never understood the language of opposites:
good, bad, male, female, right, wrong.
I'm not as easy as binary.

Sometimes ones are zeroes, zeroes ones;
sometimes the sum of my half-life
plus your wingspan equals two
parts vodka, two parts gin, two parts
make a whole like the one in my head—

what were you thinking when you had me
take English as my mother tongue?
I may not mean to say what's on my mind,
but I do. When I am silent, I am saying
exactly what I mean, and I mean business,

the business of bees. I serve myself
and save the labor of the middle man,
my mouth, who tires of forgetting who wanted which
flavor of ice cream, flavor of coffee, flavor
of favor: words as party treats, words worth

the paper they get printed on. Don't forget to flush
that taste out of your mouth, from which
spill the family jewels of wisdom you call speech.
Forget the rest, I forgot to take the test,
I forgot the answers on that sheet

they handed out before class: A-B-A-B-C-D-E
R-U-A-W-A-R-E/T-H-A-T-U-R-C/H-E-A-T-I-N-G ?

I wrote this next line on the inside of my wrist:
In 1776 someone wrote something down so well
that people went to war over words like "tax"

and "free"—the same things around April
and Christmas. Binary codes don't work for me
because I refuse to work for such insulting wages:
Give me more zeroes—then you're talking.
Give me chocolate, vanilla, strawberry, *and* Neapolitan.

Give me a question worth my time:
"To be or not to be," that's one
worth answering *after* thinking about it,
and after you think long and hard enough
about any question, you realize that truth

doesn't need to be explained, and nothing else
is worth mentioning, and nothing else goes unchallenged,
and nothing else is everything else, and nothing is everything,
and being is nothingness, and the universe expands,
plumps up when you cook it, explodes in your stomach

like Pop Rocks and Coke, like rice thrown
at wedding pigeons, like the head of a man
who thinks too goddamn much. Give me a quiet
room, and I'll send you blank tapes for Christmas,
which you'll play with the volume up, wondering what I meant.

Book

And before I knew it, we were across the river:
There you were, reading from a book with cum-
stained pages. The Outlaw Josie Wales. Tell
me a story, I said, without knowing why, or
what kind of stories are in such books, books
read and re-read, not to children, but maybe
to the children of the heart.
                              Here inside her
insides, it is dark and warm. Bedroom full of
blankets. Nestling theory. Belongings from
collections of greatest-hits singers. Beyond
the river, where the ducks walk, it is just
as warm and weary as the bedroom. As her.

Shall we begin, then, at the beginning? How
far (back) are you willing to go? (Your grin
just now is dark and evil and you have more
teeth than sharks, row on row) No, I say,
don't tell me any stories I haven't heard
before. Just tell me the name on the cover.

Judge my book. I am a sinner and my penance
is sex. Ask me about my crimes. Shop for me
at home. Tell *me* some stories, little girl,
and I'll braid your hair while you whisper
about monsters and the deep, deep blue of
the moon and the sea. All shadows. All busy
reflecting off themselves. Cover me up. Soon.

(You can bank on me baby I kind of wish you
would) (Eat my trust) (Let me, let go of me)
(Get over what? You? Darling, I never had
you to get over.) (Look me up, I'm in the
dictionary) (Whooping Cough) (How many be-
longings does one person need) (Need me?
Don't. Please. I couldn't stand the pressure)

Once upon a time there were all these little
girls, and they were playing dress-up, and Miss

Jenny always got to be Cinderella, and no one
wanted to be ugly, or wicked, though most little
girls are both when they're around other little
girls, so everyone else was girls at the ball,
and the little spook thought the ivory slip
with the lace detailing at the top was the most
beautiful dress in the closet! and you can't
wear a slip for a dress! Let her, she looks
(pretty/ugly/weird) and I like this dress.

Every Tuesday, a man (David) takes his
shovel to the backyard, but no one really
believes him. On Wednesdays, Priscilla puts
her ducks in a row. This Thursday, the first
of many deaths in our family will happen.

Rice is so good! So easy to cook! and so cheap!

Let's get back to the situation at hand.
There's me and you on some weird road-
trip or sideshow or haunted house. You
are holding a book in your hand and we
argue over the wisdom of telling stories.
You keep bringing up sex and I keep get-
ting flustered or distracted. A fuck
is a fuck. If it quacks like a fuck, that is.

Our sponsor lifts his head, and his ears
are weary and soft, as if they were spoilt.
There is a little girl, crying. There
is a little butter, melting. What's your
story about now, pumpkinhead? You're a little
teapot. I could buy a railroad with the look
on your face. I could tame a python with the
soup she made last night. Pharaohs and bogs.

Darling, darling, kneeling before me, I know
you so well, I know you so warm and wet and
soft, softer than angel snow, and smaller —
lift me up brandish me before you before you
die my death for me can we glow in the dark —

let's us try. (try as she may, the little
cat still clung to the tree) trymeflyme, babe.

They say most of what she says is based on
random neuron firings. She has no control
over her mouth or fledgling spirits.
One of the tragedies of medicine, my dear:
the mentally incontinent: They truly cannot
help running at the mouth, and the mess
that they make is just as stinky and yellow—

I have a gift for you. You don't have one yet.

Darling, she says, taking a long drag
from the cigarette in the holder, *I am the death*
you want to die a thousand times. I am the
haven you'll hide in again and again. Each
step you take away from me will only pull
you closer in the end. And I am the end.

(but the book what about the book)

He looks me (you look me) straight in the eye,
stroking a page from the book. Title obscured
and author obscurer. Your hands are scratching
textured ointments from someone's lovers. You
look away at some howling moon and here we are:
You, me, and a book. And that's what you say.
And the book is us. And there is no thing we
haven't dreamed. And one of us made the other
up. And the sheets are stained with cum. And
one of us has been conceived or deceived
or received. And we are happy. And the night
is wet. And the moon is dark. And we are young
and small and twisting in the wind.

(Hold the wind. Hold the wind. Hold the wind.)

Don't I Know You

Excuse me, sir, your hat
blocks my view of the screen.
Oh. Don't I know you?
Have I seen your face somewhere
Or is it just one of those faces?
Are you someone who looks familiar

To everyone who sees you? Are you familiar
With the cowboy wearing the black hat,
The black horse, the bandanna covering his face?
It's just a smoke screen.
He's robbing a train. Sometime. Somewhere.
He reminds me of you.

But I don't think I know you.
The smell of lemons: Familiar:
You've heard this song somewhere
Before, worn this soft hat
A million other times. I'm screening
My calls. Today I can't face

People, much less facts, much less face
The faces that I think I know. You
Happen to own a silkscreen
Of a street scene, familiar.
Worshipped: a brush stroke. A hat.
Faces of women, of men. Somewhere

Right now, a woman somewhere
Painstakingly creates her face
With a set of brushes. She wears a hat
When she doesn't have time to be you.
She doesn't have time to be familiar.
We're at an important screening,

You, she, and I, of a silver-screen
Western retrospective. In California somewhere,
A man remarks how familiar

Every movie seems these days. His face
Is expressionless. He could be you.
He doesn't wear a hat;

He screens his friends for hat-
Wearers or shoe-polishers. Familiar faces
Become familiar names. Somewhere I lost you.

In-Just Spring

It's spring,
    and the young lovers
    are breeding in the streets
like cockroaches. Like rats.

Everything is green,
    is a warm bowl of envy and collard greens,
    is a field where little girls hunt four-leaf
        clovers, find daisies, and make
        their first chains.

A strawberry plant is a time bomb,
    is a dandelion,
    is an allergy.

Dolls cry real tears from the neglect
    of reason and of bees.

Farmers sow kisses in the fields,
    and the potatoes are so far away
    they aren't real. They are ideas,
    and the ideal potato
    becomes french fries eventually.

Farmers sow kisses, and boys sow fingers
    that ripen into doubt, wishes,
    doubt, children, gods.

Spring is when cries of "Oh, God" in the night
    are answered with signs
    made of sweat and gossip.

Spring is a temptress,
    is Pandora's box of chocolate hopes,
    is a many-fingered thing with wings,
    is a candied violet, melting.

Spring crawls up your leg,
    slips under your pants,

catches behind your knee,
and stings you repeatedly
until you smash it.
You never smash it.

Drunk on venom and regret,
    You run into the street naked and yowling,
    "Look at me! Somebody love me!
    Look what I have for you!
    Look! Somebody love me,
    Somebody help me,
    I am drowning in all this!"

Spring is for cleaning. Be careful,
    or in your zeal for renewal,
    you will throw away spring itself,
    like a balled-up ticket stub
    with the name of no movie
    printed on it.

Spring is for cleaning out.
    Spring rolls out with a tide and fog
    and washes back in, filled
    like a vacuum cleaner bag
    with dust and heat and bugs
    and regrets.

Spring is the mattress tag
    you ripped off the bed
    and forgot.

Spring is when all forms of reason
    are rounded up
    and summarily shot.

Rolled into Iowa City fresh out of four years of liberal arts college on the East Coat. Poured myself from the catering business into a bartending job in one of the trailer park bars. Let me explain this phrase. There are two kinds of bars in Iowa City: college bars that UIowa students get trashed in, and local bars, which locals get drunk in and the college students call, without exception, dives.

Memories was a dive. I called it a trailer park bar because 90 percent of my clientele lived in one of Iowa City's bustling tin can condos, generally at Hill Top Trailer Court. The customers all knew each other, what and how much one another drank, and what to do to piss one another off. As a college graduate, I had to learn the art of not responding to slurs about dykes or niggers without getting threatened with getting fired for getting in their business. "Larry's my friend, and he owns this bar!" Trying to stay out of conversations was harder, though. "Hey, come over here and tell us who's right!"

One of the regulars, a guy who was known as Fargie, recited his address every night on his way out the door. "76 Hill Top Trailer Court. Just knock and come on in. And wear those leather pants!"

Good night, Fargie.

Fargie was one of the most harmless of the regulars. No felonies, I mean. He and his cohorts worked at the recycling plant, or the Proctor & Gamble factory, or the tire shop, or some other honest working-class working stiff job. Many of them had been to jail or rehab at least once. One of them, Bill, was the half-brother of one of the other bartenders as well as the right-hand man of a strong arm who was the closest thing Iowa City had to the Mob. Bill's favorite line was "Where did you get that mouth?"

Good night, Bill.

Bill had done time in a tiger cage in Vietnam and in state prison for manslaughter. He had amazing blue eyes, and his favorite drink was called the Landmine, which consisted of a shot of tequila loaded with Tabasco sauce. That was nearly the fanciest drink I ever poured in Memories. It was a beer bar whose top shelf brand was Corona. Four beers on tap, two of them Old Style and Old Style Light. Most of the mixed drinks were of the 7-and-7 or screwdriver variety. And I poured a lot of whiskey.

Jim and Jackie, the other two bartenders (who were married to each other), taught me the value of a clean bar, a good game of darts, and a tall glass of whiskey and coke. Pour yourself a Coke at the beginning of your shift. First whiskey drink you make, give your glass a nudge. Keep it filled like that all night and you won't get tired or tense. Jackie had a lot of bad tattoos, was a self-professed "fence-sitter," and could break up a fight just by looking at you funny.

Good night, Jackie.

Jackie's husband, Jim, kept a hairbrush behind the bar and had big bug eyes that stuck out of his aging rock star face. Jim would periodically kick whiskey, as would a lot of the other patrons when they got so far gone that they had a fight or a fling with someone who wouldn't ordinarily register as more than another regular. One of these whiskey-quitters was Janine, a fat girl with mean eyes and whiskers on her chin. To celebrate, she drank Yukon Jack, a whiskey liqueur with a burn and a smooth slide down the back of the throat. Janine had a lot of friends who only really appreciated her truck.

Good night, Janine.

Janine was a gossiper who'd two-time her own mother if it meant she got to deliver a scoop. She often scooped both about or to the owner, Larry. Larry drank Old Style in a can, played a mean game of darts, and installed videocameras behind the bar. My first day of work, Larry told me that I'd have to learn how to cut people off. No matter how strange it may seem, it's illegal to serve liquor to a person who's drunk. Bartenders do it all the time, but they need to learn when a customer really is too drunk to drink. They need to serve a glass of water or coke and call a cab or secure a ride with a non-drinking patron (there were several regulars who only drank sodas). Larry also told me that when he and his girlfriend, Roxie, were too drunk, I would need to cut them off, too.

Right, Larry.

There came a day when I walked in and could tell that Larry and Roxie had been occupying their posts at the end of the bar for the majority of the day. A lot of the customers come in as soon as they leave work and don't leave until way into the evening, often ordering pizza from next door to tide them over while they demolished most of a case of beer, often without any visible effects on their affects. Not this time. Roxie was slurring her speech so bad she sounded like a crackhead. She was nodding off into her beer, and when she got up to play darts, she was throwing towards the wall, but nowhere near the vicinity of the dartboard. Roxie was a dart league champ.

You okay, Roxie?

They'd been fighting. They fought a lot. Larry ordered another round and I told him that Roxie was too drunk to have another beer. He ordered the beer and ordered me to serve it. I refused. I called a cab and told them to get in and they dismissed it. And then he dismissed me.

"You serve her that beer or you quit," he said.

"That's damn illegal and you know it," I said.

"Then you're fired," he said.

I got my shit and left. They got an ex-bartender, also drunk, to finish my shift. She stole $80 from the till and blamed it on me. I left that dysfunctional family of bar flies there. When I checked in occasionally over the next year, they were all still there, all still drunk, all still nodding into their drinks and barely recognizing me, not at all recognizing themselves in their friends sent to detox for repeated DWI.

Me, I stopped drinking on the job, because I stopped bartending. I recognized myself in the bottom of the glass. I haven't been there in years.

Dear Jay

Dear Jay,

I almost died this morning, and that had nothing to do with you. I was going to write to you about getting lost on the way out of Las Vegas. Not that I didn't follow your instructions, because I did. But I got confused about driving north in order to go south in order to go north again, so I exited and looked at a map. After I discovered that I really did need to go north off the bat, I drove around and was pleased to discover that my find-the-highway instincts actually worked. I made it to the requisite interstate and thought that that was my road excitement for the rest of the day.

Timing is a funny thing. If you leave a minute or two earlier or later, if you take a second more or less at a light or changing lanes or getting gas, things might turn out completely differently.

I had almost cleared Nevada heading south on I-15. I was trucking along in the left lane, enjoying myself, looking at the beautiful day, passing tanker trucks—you know, freeway stuff. Up ahead I saw a cloud of dust, and a second later, a van emerged from it. The van was heading towards me, in the left lane. I should mention that the median strip at this point on the highway is a steep ditch at least ten feet deep. I thought I was imagining things; I thought the sun was in my eyes; I thought I was hallucinating; I thought he was going to stop; I thought I was going to die.

I couldn't change lanes because of the aforementioned tanker truck, and I couldn't stop because the person behind me hadn't seen anything yet. I slowed down as much as I could and then bit the bullet and merged into a semi. We bumped tires, and he sped up to give me the space behind him. At that instant, the van again descended into the median from which it came.

I stopped on the highway shoulder for a minute, trying to see the van and if it was killing anyone. No one else stopped. I pulled off the next exit at the welcome station and reported the incident to the police. A few minutes after I got back on the highway, I saw an ambulance headed toward the spot I had left.

I'm glad I'm still alive. I had several near misses on this trip, none of them my fault, and right now I think I'll be happiest never to enter a car again (or at least, not for a few days). If they catch the guy, I may have to return to Nevada for court.

My life, if you're wondering, did not flash before my eyes.

Regards,

J. Tarin Towers
looking@tarin.com

J. Tarin Towers, 27, was born and raised in rural Maryland. She earned a degree from Washington College in Chestertown, Maryland. Her piece, *Mission Poem*, appears in the *Pushcart Prize XXIII: Best of the Small Presses* anthology. Towers is the author of *The Dreamweaver Visual QuickStart Guide* (Peachpit Press), and has contributed to more than a dozen books about computers and the Internet. Her website address is www.tarin.com. She currently resides in San Francisco.

Manic D Press Books

Po Man's Child. *Marci Blackman*. $12.95

The Underground Guide to Los Angeles. *Pleasant Gehman, ed*. $13.95

Flashbacks and Premonitions. *Jon Longhi*. $11.95

The Forgiveness Parade. *Jeffrey McDaniel*. $11.95

The Sofa Surfing Handbook: a guide for modern nomads. *edited by Juliette Torrez*. $11.95

Abolishing Christianity and other short pieces. *Jonathan Swift*. $11.95

Growing Up Free In America. *Bruce Jackson*. $11.95

Devil Babe's Big Book of Fun! *Isabel Samaras*. $11.95

Dances With Sheep. *Keith Knight*. $11.95

Monkey Girl. *Beth Lisick*. $11.95

Bite Hard. *Justin Chin*. $11.95

Next Stop: Troubletown. *Lloyd Dangle*. $10.95

The Hashish Man and other stories. *Lord Dunsany*. $11.95

Forty Ouncer. *Kurt Zapata*. $11.95

The Unsinkable Bambi Lake. *Bambi Lake with Alvin Orloff*. $11.95

Hell Soup: the collected writings of Sparrow 13 LaughingWand. $8.95

Revival: spoken word from Lollapalooza 94. *edited by Torrez, Belile, Baron & J. Joseph*. $12.95

The Ghastly Ones & Other Fiendish Frolics. *Richard Sala*. $9.95

The Underground Guide to San Francisco. *Jennifer Joseph, ed*. $10.95

King of the Roadkills. *Bucky Sinister*. $9.95

Alibi School. *Jeffrey McDaniel*. $8.95

Signs of Life: channel-surfing through '90s culture. *edited by J. Joseph & L. Taplin*. $12.95

Beyond Definition: new writing from gay & lesbian s. f. *Blackman & Healey, eds*. $10.95

Love Like Rage. *Wendy-o Matik* $7.00

The Language of Birds. *Kimi Sugioka* $7.00

The Rise and Fall of Third Leg. *Jon Longhi* $9.95

Specimen Tank. *Buzz Callaway* $10.95

The Verdict Is In. *edited by Kathi Georges & Jennifer Joseph* $9.95

Elegy for the Old Stud. *David West* $7.00

The Back of a Spoon. *Jack Hirschman* $7.00

Mobius Stripper. *Bana Witt* $8.95

Baroque Outhouse/Decapitated Head of a Dog. *Randolph Nae* $7.00

Graveyard Golf and other stories. *Vampyre Mike Kassel* $7.95

Bricks and Anchors. *Jon Longhi* $8.00

The Devil Won't Let Me In. *Alice Olds-Ellingson* $7.95

Greatest Hits. *edited by Jennifer Joseph* $7.00

Lizards Again. *David Jewell* $7.00

The Future Isn't What It Used To Be. *Jennifer Joseph* $7.00

Please add $2.50 to all orders for postage and handling.

Manic D Press • Box 410804 • San Francisco CA 94141 USA

info@manicdpress.com   www.manicdpress.com

Distributed to the trade
in the US & Canada by Publishers Group West
in the UK & Europe by Turnaround Distribution